GW00712317

CHRISTIAN MARRIAGE TODAY

CHRISTIAN MARRIAGE TODAY

Edited by Klaus Demmer and
Aldegonde Brenninkmeijer-Werhahn

The Catholic University of America Press
Washington, D.C.

Copyright © 1997
The Catholic University of America Press
All rights reserved
Printed in the United States of America

Cover and title page illustration credit: *Song of Songs* in *Drawings and Texts: Shraga Weil,* published by Sifriat Poalim, 1958.

The paper used in this publication meets the minimum requirements of American National Standards for Information Science—Permanence of Paper for Printed Library materials, ANSI z39.48-1984.
∞

LIBRARY OF CONGRESS CATALOGING-IN-PUBLICATION DATA

Christian marriage today : edited by Klaus Demmer and
  Aldegonde Brenninkmeijer-Werhahn.
      p.   cm.
  "Results of a symposium, held in Brussels in 1994"—Pref.
  Includes bibliographical references and index.
  1. Marriage—Religious aspects—Catholic Church—
Congresses. 2. Catholic Church—Doctrines—Congresses.
  I. Demmer, Klaus, 1931– . II. Brenninkmeijer-Werhahn,
Aldegonde.
  BX2250.C5547   1996
  248.4—dc20
  96-28093
  ISBN 0-8132-0876-9 (alk. paper)
  ISBN 0-8132-0877-7 (pbk.: alk. paper)

CONTENTS

Preface / vii

1. The Origin of an Idea / 1
   Klaus Demmer

2. Marriage as Seen by Christian
   Anthropology / 13
   Jörg Splett

3. The Many Changes in the Concept of Christian
   Marriage and the Family throughout
   History / 25
   Michel Rouche

4. Married Persons: God's Chosen People / 38
   Ladislas Örsy, S.J.

5. Marriage as a Sacrament towards a
   New Theological Conceptualization / 55
   Carlo Rocchetta

Contributors / 81

Bibliography / 83

Index / 87

PREFACE

This book is the result of a symposium held in Brussels in 1994 on the theme of "Christian Marriage Today." It was organized by the International Academy for Marital Spirituality (INTAMS).

INTAMS is an initiative that focuses on the varying forms of lived marriages in different cultures and religions. In particular INTAMS considers the Christian marriage and its vocation. In all religions and cultures, human beings seek happiness and desire a meaningful life. Similarly married couples, whether entering marriage or already married, strive to live marriage to the fullest.

Scholars and experts from more than eight countries are working in the Academy. The many facets of marriage can only be learned from various disciplines, including anthropology, economics, history, law, literature and art, medicine, philosophy, political science, psychology, sociology, theology, etc. The scientific research and the lived reality of marriage complement and enrich each other. INTAMS tries therefore to integrate theoretical reflection with praxis of marriage.

After some years of deep and fundamental reflection, this group of Christians, men and women, married and unmarried, and some of them priests, religious and celibates, started in 1989 to organize yearly colloquia treating the various questions concerning marriage. In January 1994 the first international symposium was held on the subject of "Christian Marriage Today."

Why this book?

The question of whether we should make our work accessible to a wider circle has often been considered. Not only could we share our work with others, but we would have the opportunity of entering into a dialogue with an even larger forum. As a result, this book is our effort to share and expand the dialogue on the topic of Christian marriage.

The opening paper of this symposium is given by the moral theologian Klaus Demmer. A co-initiator and member of the Board of Trustees of INTAMS, he lectures in the Gregoriana in Rome. In "The Origin of an Idea" he reflects on the initial concepts, concerns, and development of INTAMS.

Jörg Splett, a philosophical anthropologist from Sankt Georgen in Germany, brings forward the Christian understanding of man and woman as human beings who themselves are searching for meaning for their existence. Personal love preserves the distance and the duality of I and Thou for the sake of the unity of love and togetherness of a mutual I-am-Yours. This distinction between I and Thou is the task of *modesty* respecting the partner's mystery. It is the only way in which *freedom* can really be free.

Michel Rouche, a historian from the Sorbonne in Paris, describes the manifold concepts of marriage and family throughout European history. He starts with the Roman Empire, continues through the settlement of the Germanic tribes in the West up to the reign of Charlemagne. Rouche then describes the influence of Christianity, especially of the monks' views on marriage and the Church authorities who began to create a new language of respect and esteem for the love between man and woman. Finally he comments on the understanding of marriage during the Renaissance and briefly considers the period after the Council of Trent up to our century.

Ladislas Örsy, well-known professor of canon law in the United States, speaks of the sacrament of marriage as a sign with a special vocation. Man and woman in union reveal the image of their Creator more perfectly together than one of them could alone. Is God the initiator in this dramatic event? What does God think about marriage, and how is He present throughout their lives, when husband and wife promise lifelong fidelity? How does He assist married life, and what is the practical outcome for marriage in spirituality, in liturgy, and for the church law?

Carlo Rocchetta is professor of dogmatical theology in Florence and in this article follows Vatican II's terminological shift from marriage as a "contract" to marriage as a "covenant." He traces three main guidelines for a new theological conceptualization of marriage as a sacrament. With the conception of sacramental matrimony in terms of *vocation, consecration,* and *communion,* the marital covenant is understood consequently as a "real symbol" of an ecclesial gesture and as a sign in history of the irrevocable love of God towards humankind.

INTAMS is always looking for opportunities to carry out its work. Therefore let me thank Rev. Msgr. John F. Wippel and Dr. David J. McGonagle who have been so kind in helping me in the process of publishing this book. I would also like to thank Rev. Prof. Enda McDonagh from Maynooth, Ireland, a member of our Board of Trustees, who helped in the translation of these contributions. My gratitude also goes to the INTAMS' staff, Thomas Knieps-Port le Roi, Ilse Cornu, and Rita Demil.

In conclusion, I especially would like to thank Professor Klaus Demmer for his co-editorship of this book but even more for his advice and continuous encouragement. And finally I thank my loving husband for his patience and unending counsel. INTAMS is the fruit of 30 years of blessed and deeply experienced marriage.

Aldegonde Brenninkmeijer-Werhahn

CHRISTIAN MARRIAGE TODAY

Klaus Demmer

1   THE ORIGIN OF AN IDEA

Events, such as this symposium, are not the result of one moment, however privileged; they are preceded by multiple ramifications and timid attempts. There certainly was an idea at the origin of it, but it had no clearly defined contour; it was struggling for its own profile, needing a multiplicity of conversations growing like ripples in ever increasing circles, reaching others within the same frame. Now, ideas are never the product of mere spirit; rather, pressing and at times oppressive experiences bring their influence to bear on the person immediately responsible for the idea. Not without reason theology as a science speaks of *Sitz im Leben*.

The same is true here and today. This intermingling of idea and experience has its reference point in an ecclesiastical, social, and very personal emergency: for the large majority of people, marriage is the normal state of life. In spite of this, both the Church and society fail in providing fundamental help to make marriage succeed. This is a particularly sad experience when it comes to official pronouncements of the Church. When the concept of a generally successful life is linked with the choice and realization of an actual state of life, there is a notorious lack of guidance from the Church: committed Christians want to be guided by the Church in understanding how marriage as a sacrament can be lived as a very personal vocation in the context of a secularized, ephemeral, and amorphous world.

Christians feel helpless when faced with the bombastic pallor of theological theses or formulations of the Church's teaching authority. It is all well-intended but does not reach its target, namely the everyday life of a married couple in a world full of constraints and trivialities. Married people have no idea that theology is a store of wisdom for life, having its roots in human lives that have suffered and stood the test, thus providing fertile soil, as it were, for abstract thoughts. There a bridge has to be built. Theology is always produced from original situations; the theologian is an existential thinker before s/he tries to systematize her/his thoughts. S/he tries to explain at the level of concepts the story of her/his own life, and thus s/he acquires the skill to take up the thought-through lives of married people, casting them in a communicable theological form. When married people feel that something is wanting in Church life, their own experience sparks an appeal to theology: is theology, with due respect for the loftiness of its thinking, really in touch with life, or is it no more than an erudite collection of fairy tales, hurting no one, but not helping anyone either in times of great need? Texts of the Church's teaching authority have only so much life in them as the theology of the moment allows them to have.

The Church's teaching authority situates marriage in the family as its principal context, so much so that the interpenetration of the two has become a current paradigm for the official mode of thinking of the Church. There is not, however, sufficient awareness of the fact that genetically marriage precedes the family, that success of the family depends on success of the marriage, and that, especially today, the marriage partnership takes up a considerable amount of time. Both teaching authority and theology must take these realities of the relationship between marriage and the family into account, otherwise their lofty perorations fail to reach men and women of our time. This absence of a *Sitz im Leben*, characteristic of theological reflection today, results necessarily in a vacuum: committed Christians do not recognize themselves in today's theological pronouncements; they get the uncomfortable feeling of being passive subjects of a purely theoretical pastoral ministry in which the ideas they contribute, be they ever so modest, do not count at all. And yet they too, as committed Christians, are theologians, responsible and capable partners of the teaching authority within the *communio* of the Church. Their life experience is—at least in embryo—already the beginning of a theory that possesses the undeniable advantage of being able to claim for itself practical clarity and, consequently, a wealth of facets. The professional theologian takes this life experience up, reflects on it with the help of his/her professional criteria, and hands it back to his/her contemporaries. Looked at in this way, theology is a partnership of contemporaries on the level of responsible thinking, and it needs the contribution of the committed Christian.

Theology that is based on experience—and here again we recognize an important factor in the previous history—has a spiritual component. There is no lack of high-level theology of marriage, whether in the field of dogma, exegesis, or pastoral care. And yet there is an important element missing of which married couples are the exclusive victims. The best theology of marriage confronts its own limits where there is a question of putting abstract theological thinking through the filter of spiritual experience. After all, Christian marriage is not only a privileged human and moral field of self-realization; as a sacramental vocation, it takes part in the transformation of life that was begun in baptism. In this way Christian marriage penetrates into the inscrutable of the mystery of the triune God, thus giving rise to a unique self-awareness that should be jointly and responsibly conceptualized, shared in conversation, and witnessed to in prayer. Life's wisdom needs to enter into a symbiosis with the insight of faith.

Christians undergo the same experiences as non-Christians, but on no account do Christians want to give up the courage to be different. The manifold leveling pressures of a pluralist society—the contradiction is only apparent—should not penetrate into the innermost area of marriage; rather, a contrasting program should be developed. There is a sense here of a spiritual emergency that constitutes a challenge for the Church. Prior to the symposium, it was clear in the preparatory conversations that the concept of spirituality lends itself to all sorts of misconceptions. It can degenerate into a vogue word, or it may even suggest the secret and exclusive, if not sectarian. As a result we need to reflect on the best elements in theological tradition. Our thinking is purest when it exposes itself directly and defenselessly to the brusqueness and even severity of the gospel and tries the uncalculated, noble deed in ever renewed attempts. Spirituality is far removed from a hidden life without risks; it feels the urgency of public testimony.

Genesis of the Symposium

This symposium is the climax of a series of colloquia which marked a kind of preliminary phase. During these colloquia, the number of participants grew, and the profile of the main theme under discussion became visibly clearer. A multiple critical filter was needed to bring what, so far, were vague thoughts to greater clarity and give the theme its own orbit. From the beginning we were conscious that only a dialectical interaction of situation analysis and reflection analysis could help us achieve results. And this took place in various steps, year by year. No wonder the consciousness of the problem grew more intense and the aim of our work became ever more concrete!

Let us recall the characteristic phases, reconstructing the genesis of the thought-process, because it will make the outcome of the symposium so much clearer. In this way history is dealt with systematically. The first logical step was to describe the phenomenon of marriage in modern society as it is characterized by a new division of labor. After all, even the most abstract thought reflects a given social situation. The most important question was, if and how far the change in the role-consciousness between men and women would have its effect on the form and contents of both the Church's teaching authority and the pastoral ministry. In contrast to the traditional cliché of man as the head and woman as the heart of the family (Pius XI), marriage in contemporary society is defined, as a belated product of the Enlightenment, by strict equality between the two participants. As a result, women's self-awareness has been undergoing a profound change. Women now understand themselves to be equal to men in education and development; no wonder, therefore, that this leads to changes in the balance of power within marriage.

Women are often no longer dependent for better or for worse on men as their only source of income; if needs be, they can fend for themselves. This new reality has its effect on the way married couples cope with crisis situations: a self-conscious woman will not continue a broken marriage simply to maintain a social façade or to fulfill a martyr's complex. She possesses the economic muscle power to stand on her own two feet. In addition, the sexual relationship experiences the impact of this change. Marriage duty very often used to be the women's burden; they were the ones to accede, the men could demand. In Western culture this model has resulted in a double morality. Now, however, this changing relationship means that men must learn to adjust, and they may find it more difficult to accept the new situation. As a result, tensions may easily become exacerbated and especially in cases where men and women are professionally engaged in different worlds. In this situation, partners often find it difficult to reserve "prime time" for each other in order to manage their diverging interests and emotional bonds and to call each other back to one another. It is not infidelity but a creeping alienation that most often poisons marriage. A sensible pastoral worker should take note of that.

Right from the start of the colloquia, the participants were aware that situation analyses could only serve to provide the orientation for the alternative program. The courage to be different longs for a spiritual profile, tailor-made for the committed Christian. It is quite true that you cannot just make up a spirituality of marriage, but you can kindle it and nurse it assiduously. The colloquia participants all agreed that committed married Christians have the same life experiences as other people, yet these Christians feel the need for an interpretive key that would prevent their marriage from getting swamped by trivialities. For this a style of conduct is needed that clearly distances itself from its surroundings; one must not allow one's conduct to be dictated by current and often faddish systems of value. Marriage constitutes an inner sanctum—theology speaks of a home church—which gives rise to an unmistakable physiognomy. The voices of Christians expecting guidance from the Church become more vociferous, people are on the lookout for new and convincing models, for examples that stimulate and inspire. A purely normative ethic that insists monotonously on duty is here no longer sufficient: it can only partly do justice to the multifaceted nature of life. What married couples need is a conciliatory ethic which they experience as inviting. What is needed is not a normative ethic but an attitudinal one.

To do more justice to these demands, we needed more reflection. Where in present-day theology do we find promising starting-points from which we can pick up and develop? Assistance could come from moral theology, as it has as its primary task to be at the service of life, by fusing life experience, life's wisdom and theological insight into a creative synthesis. In *Familiaris Consortio* marriage is described as a vocation; this text from the Church's teaching authority could serve as a sign of commitment to a spiritual theology of marriage. How can marriage be understood—and lived—as a strictly personal vocation? That moral theology, with respect to this question, depends on the collaboration of other theological disciplines is obvious. But this challenge must be taken up, if the purpose of the colloquia is to be fulfilled.

What can moral theology contribute from its own perspective? It can certainly lay claim to the methodological advantage that its starting point lies in the lived experience of marriage, without a strong emphasis on dogmatic premises, although the latter are implicitly accepted. Moral theology looks on the decision to marry as an irrevocable decision for life with which the partners identify themselves unreservedly and which, as it were, takes the place of their unique selves and guarantees a meaningful and successful life's story. Persons who enter into such a decision for life project themselves towards an open future. They do not know what the future will bring them but simply cherish the hope of being able to cope with all the vicissitudes of life. A decision for life is at first unfinished, comparable to a seed. In the course of a life's history, it develops to its full riches and finds its completion in death. A decision for life does not simply fall from the sky; we need a lifetime to work at it, protecting and looking after it like a tender plant. The partner is certainly experienced as an unmerited gift, but at the same time s/he has to be conquered. A decision for life is a lifelong task that is carried out in fidelity to oneself and to the traveling companion of one's common history, two-in-one, finding its final fulfillment in the resurrection. Its perseverance is the anticipatory image of eternity.

At this point in the thinking of the colloquia participants, a connection was made with the other theological disciplines; the moral theologian is, after all, not on a solo trip. It was a question of opening up the riches of the word "vocation," and a reflection on a liturgical level, both from the Western and the Eastern Church, was able to provide the first viewpoints worth considering. They were connected with the formula of "consecration." "Consecration" is the liturgical expression of "vocation." The *lex orandi* is the original expression of the *lex credendi;* the liturgical celebration of the sacraments is the privileged hermeneutical place of the Church's understanding of the faith. There was consensus among the colloquia participants that there was a need for research into the history of the liturgy in order to satisfy the primary objective of the group. In addition, biblical and dogmatic theology had been asked for their opinions, and they came with their specific contributions. Both sides were able to make quite clear that an understanding of the sacraments that is narrowed down to the purely juridical reflects only very partially the Church's tradition of faith and could even be said to distort it.

When the Second Vatican Council in its Pastoral Constitution comes to a change of paradigms by replacing the idea of contract by that of covenant, we have to remember that the Bible prepared the way for this. It is precisely the moving images of the Old Testament that provide present-day theology of marriage with the themes for a deeper reflection. The alliance between Yahweh and his chosen people is seen in the image of a marriage, an alliance in which unbreakable fidelity and tender love are intertwined. This image allows us to gain a better understanding of marriage itself, though in this context marriage is no more than a reflection of this archetype. Yet this first remark is not the last. Theology of the covenant cannot be conceived without a corresponding theology of history. The history of the chosen people cannot be reduced to the outcome of certain dramatic events; what is far more prominent is a drama of the spirit. The purpose of all the events is to get an ever clearer understanding of the pure and undefinable transcendence of God. The history of God's people is a history of the ongoing self-revelation of God, which is something pertaining to human thought. The application of the theology of history to marriage simply forced itself upon the Old Testament authors. Marriage can be compared to a history of the spirit; all events serve the purpose of giving the thinking about God its unique form. Marriage is a history of entering into God. A marriage, as a vocation and an alliance, develops, in the course of the time given to it, its own very specific theology of history.

It is logical that at this point the dogmatic theologian takes up the story. Although insights into present-day sacramental theology have been updated, it was nonetheless the purpose of the colloquia participants to come to a new discovery of marriage as a sacrament for the practice of life. Thus it was necessary to begin reflecting on the history of dogma that started with the Council of Trent and has continued through Vatican II. It is a lasting merit of the latter council to have broken open the strait-jacket of juridical thinking. Marriage is doubtless also a pact or treaty that is entered into freely by two persons equal before the law; this norm must retain the importance it has achieved historically. But its theological reality requires a wider explanation: the two-in-one character of the couple is a gift of sharing in the life and interchange of love of the Blessed Trinity. All dimensions of married life, from its sexual to its mental and spiritual expression, are inserted into this mystery and thus are inwardly transformed, that is to say, given new meaning; they have been given a new ontological and therefore anthropological quality. In this way, the sacrament of marriage is a sign of life of God in the deathly decadence of our time, it opens up a field of innovative practice. We can rightly expect that the human quality of man, and the whole spectrum of his experiences and insights, are in good hands when we entrust them to the theologian, but this expectation can only be fulfilled if the theologian reflects on her/his best theological traditions, and if s/he realizes that theology is made in the midst of life and that it is precisely there that it affects people.

Theological thinking is found in its purest form where it confronts everyday life, so much was clear to everyone concerned. Psychology and pastoral experience within a particular situation must explain phenomena. The danger of resorting to rather useless abstractions threatens the theologian at every step, and this has to be avoided at any price, especially with respect to the problems under discussion. Of great concern is the reality of marriages that fail: What are the decisive reasons for this, and—leaving theological commonplaces aside—what can be done to prevent failure? It is no doubt legitimate to speak of structures of sin. But what do they look like in the concrete? Here the psychologist could explain how, behind every decision for life, there is hidden a life's destiny that at times becomes painfully clear. When people have been conditioned by oppressive experiences, especially as children, they can be handicapped in their love. If, despite this condition, this still implies at least a minimum of assurance that a lifelong bond can be maintained, are they then really capable of choosing a partner? Or, because they are unable to break through the vicious cycle of their past, are they condemned to failure? Are they a kind of recidivists? In such situations, how far do canonical criteria really apply? So often in the pastoral ministry, there is talk of people who are unable to receive the sacraments. This sorrow is felt most deeply by those who are married. Pastoral guidance in this case must seriously reflect on its possibilities and limits; global judgments, or even condemnations, should in any case be forbidden.

Results and Expectations

Although much has had to remain unsaid, we have sketched here the most relevant phases of the genesis of this symposium. But as history can be written with a particular purpose in mind, so too has this short sketch been rendered with an aim in view: that the principal concerns manifested in the colloquia should be articulated in a number of main themes. The primary concern was to bridge the gap between theory and practice and to pass the compulsively abstract theological thinking through the critical filter of concrete life. How helpful is theology when the daily routine of the married couple develops into a tug of war, when people are facing unplanned and unforeseen challenges, or when people are even having to cope with disasters in their lives? We should remember that theological theory is religious praxis that has been reflected on and systematized; there is no clean separation of theory from praxis, both are complementary to one another. Theory saves praxis from becoming unreal, fragmented, and diffuse, the way speech saves thought from decline and obscurity. And theory makes praxis communicable, the way speech inserts thought into a spiritual exchange, which in principle is unlimited, and allows thought to take part in this exchange. As a result, one of the main concerns of the colloquia participants stands out very clearly: a platform should be established that could lead to a breakthrough: namely an encounter and a cross-fertilization of tradition with the conditions of our time.

As part of these concerns, the Church dimension of marriage is once more questioned. If it is true that marriage as a sacrament builds up the Church, then marriage has, as such, a vocation within the framework of the community of believers. Marriage is the active carrier of Christian proclamation and not simply a passive object of the Church's pastoral care. It is often said, with an appeal to Paul VI, that the lay person in his/her specific competence is a responsible partner of the Church's teaching authority. Is the same not true of marriage? Do married people not also have an official mission in the Church for which they are equipped by the reception of the sacrament, receiving a sort of *missio canonica?* On this, too, more specific and determined thinking should be undertaken than has hitherto taken place, and the colloquia so far should be a help in this.

Living marriage as a vocation means living it as a sacrament. General experience among Church members tells us that even committed couples do not develop a vital consciousness of this and that their understanding of the sacrament does not come up to the standard of present-day sacramental theology. It has not come home to them existentially that marriage is a sacrament with a "lasting" effect—as it is called in dogmatic theology—transforming all aspects of marriage, transforming man and woman in their manhood and womanhood, thus bearing an intimate relation to baptism and the Eucharist. It was the predominant objective of the colloquia up to this point to develop this insight and to open up the rich possibilities of its many facets. A sacrament is not just a thing, but rather a field of divine co-presence; it causes the two-in-one unit of the couple to become three-in-one. The partners are not lost in wonder, looking at each other, but fascinated by jointly looking towards the triune God.

All colloquia participants were aware that complaints about the breakdown of so many marriages does no good to anybody, least of all to those concerned. The reasons for the breakdown are as varied as life itself, and systematic reflection can never cover them adequately. Moreover, analyses are always only partially constructive; that is why a more productive approach to confronting the issue of failure in marriage seems to be offered by way of quiet, unobtrusive prevention. What can be done to prevent breakdown well in time? If the indissolubility of marriage is a promise, then this brings with it on the part of the Church the solemn duty to make marriage livable. Solidarity in the Church, even brotherly and sisterly love, starts with co-responsibility on the level of thought. To this demand the colloquia participants, both married and single, both lay persons and priests, felt themselves bound. A new language must be found that, with a view to the helplessness of so many people, can make clear the Christian vocation, couching it in terms of today. Salvation is never found in mediocrity but always in the acceptance of a high challenge. On this there was complete consensus.

Jörg Splett

2 MARRIAGE AS SEEN BY CHRISTIAN ANTHROPOLOGY

Traditionally, marriage fell under the guardianship of the family; however, as a result of developments, which I am not going to chronicle here, the modern nuclear family developed: the *famille conjugale* (Emil Durkheim). So it is now no longer the family which carries the responsibility for marriage, and marriage which strengthens the partners' affection for each other. On the contrary, the family now rests on the marriage, and marriage, in turn, is dependent on the personal affection between husband and wife. From different points of view this could be regretted as a threat to and an impoverishment of the human element. Nevertheless, not only is it a fact, but at the same time, it also provides an opportunity for a deeper understanding of the togetherness of husband and wife.

Called by Their Names as Men and Women

The impersonal, both inanimate and living things, are simply created by God as a direct expression of His will. But He cannot and does not want to create the human being in this way because it would be meaningless. He creates human beings through an act which presupposes and at the same time establishes their dignity, namely through invocation. Things are created through God's command; human beings through His invocation.[1]

Since even at the basis of the creation as such there is no imperfection that needs to be alleviated for the benefit of the creator, therefore God creates out of "pure generosity"[2] (rather than out of yearning, loneliness, etc., as certain theologians have written); especially humankind is called into being by God (becoming his Thou) only for one's own sake. Only thus can freedom blossom; if it were a means to an end, humankind would not be human. The creation of humankind would make even less sense if it had another purpose, such as the "preservation of the species" or a complementary "partnership," for example. However, human beings are looking for a meaning for themselves and their existence, in other words they are looking for a direction.[3] The person is called to something—depending on his or her talents—there are different possibilities. What now is the call a person receives as man or woman?

Gender is a natural destiny. In practice the specifically recognized male or female traits certainly show surprisingly wide variations which may be culturally determined: but first and foremost it is the fundamental physical differences that lie at the basis of gender. Now mind and body *(Leib)* means more than just the body *(Körper)*; it does not denote the *res extensa* (the whole shell) of the spiritual, the *res cogitans,* but rather the way in which a person really lives and breathes; therefore the biological difference between human genders also serves as an

---

1. Romano Guardini, *Welt und Person: Versuche zur christlichen Lehre vom Menschen,* 2d ed. (Würzburg, Ger.: Werkbund-Verlag, 1940), 114.

2. Jörg Splett, "Grundgesetz Freigebigkeit" in *Leben als Mit-Sein: Vom trinitarisch Menschlichem* (Frankfurt am Main: Verlag J. Knecht, 1990), esp. 112ff.

3. Against the modern view that holds that the purpose of life consists in its preservation, I may state: woman and man are the creatures who no longer value their own life if there is nothing they value more than their own life.

indication of other basic human differences.[4] It is true that there is no such thing as male or female physics or mathematics, but we definitely recognize (or should recognize) male or female philosophy, art, poetry, a different approach to faith and its reflection in theology.

It is not really possible to determine the far-reaching differences more precisely, because they are neither completely "natural," nor altogether cultural; even metaphysically they cannot be accurately pinpointed, because on the one hand they are more than "accidental," but on the other hand they do not originate in different species but are all different manifestations of the same species.

Despite what has been said above, the most straightforward approach concerns the natural destiny of "procreation."[5] The fact that this aspect has faded into the background is historically understandable; its general repression (even treating it as a taboo) is rather surprising when one considers that every living thing owes its existence to this phenomenon. Or is this precisely the reason for repressing it (and therefore also the reason why philosophers have always had a preference for speaking about death rather than birth)?[6] After all, human beings not only get the gift of life from other humans (instead of being self-made men and women), but they also owe the fact of becoming mothers/fathers to their partners and to their children.

But of course—at least here in our day and age—people do not only get married in order to procreate offspring, but be-

4. For example, Wolfgang Wickler and Uta Seibt, *Männlich Weiblich: Der grosse Unterschied und seine Folgen* (Munich: R. Piper, 1983).

5. To denounce this by putting forward egalitarian arguments regarding "homo-" and "hetero-" sexuality would mean that sexuality could only be determined by relating it to certain parts of the nervous system and nervous sensations.

6. As a contrast see (starting from Martin Heidegger) Hannah Arendt on *Natalität*, for example. Delbert Barley, *Hannah Arendt: Einführung in ihr Werk* (Freiburg: K. Alber, 1990).

cause they love each other. Even in cultures with a different orientation we find tales and myths that show this to be the true yearning of the heart. (It might be interesting to meditate on this issue with regard to the importance men and women have for each other outside marriage.[7])

Men and women are helpmates and support for each other. Antoine de Saint-Exupéry described friendship as "helping to live," and this must be the most precise description of humanity.[8] In fact, however, only exceptionally does help come about through a doubling of the self. The friend is no *alter ego*, s/he is a Thou—with all the magic of strangeness and close familiarity of such a face (see *The Song of Songs*). In the *vis-à-vis* of man and woman, we witness, first and foremost, the miracle of an astonishing and deeply affecting, all-pervading difference between two human beings: the shock of relativizing the self and all its usual assumptions.

The Self Starts out to Meet the Other

Our own self is self-evident to us, as the term says. Without any doubt the self is at the center of the I-perspective and its world: it seems to represent an absolute certainty. The perception of the other person means: to see him/her as one who sees me. This "relativizes" me in a twofold way: the "Other" draws me into a relationship and, at the same time, limits me. I am confronted with a *mysterium tremendum et fascinosum*. It is fascinating. The love-poetry of all times and regions provides eternal descriptions of this phenomenon. And yet, while it is fasci-

---

7. Dietrich von Hildebrand, "Die Bedeutung von Mann und Frau füreinander außerhalb der Ehe," in *Die Menschheit am Scheideweg* (Regensburg, Ger.: Habbel, 1954), 127–45.

8. Help: Gen. 2:18 (not only androcentric, but to be read also in the opposite direction); the word *ezer* is repeatedly used for God himself. Antoine de Saint-Exupéry, *Gesammelte Schriften* (Munich: dtv, 1978) Vol. 3, 202. The Vulgate translates *philanthropia*, meaning friendship to man, as *humanitas* (Tit. 3:4).

nating, the perception of the Other is also frightening and threatening, which explains the various defensive strategies: self-denial, belittling of the self, withdrawal and flight, and finally merging and incorporation.

Because it has a very impressive history and description, the latter response will be dealt with separately. According to the myth of Aristophanes at Plato's *Symposium,* we humans are only halves, always in search of the other half that we might join to become whole again. Life's melancholy means that it is only for fleeting moments that we can become one, following which the incomplete beings are precipitated into mourning again.

An even more radical position (even if it is not often pursued to the end) holds that to be (oneself) means, therefore, to be incomplete and unhappy; to be happy, or complete and whole, would mean no longer being (oneself), but merging or becoming incorporated into a larger unit, like rivers flowing into the sea. To love means to yearn; the fulfillment of the yearning would lead to the disappearance of the thou and the self—and would mean the end of love. Moreover, the proponents of this theory (in the same manner as the theoreticians of an a-personal mysticism) refer to a real experience: the erotic climax.

However, one cannot conceive of man or woman as half-beings, despite their dependence, but rather they are whole and independent creatures. In the same way, one cannot isolate the moment of ecstasy and then use it as a yardstick for the interpretation of human love. Rather it is a moment in the interplay of togetherness and caring in the *co-esse* of two independent people. In their oneness they are joyfully able to "realize" this togetherness, that is, they can experience and achieve it, in the blissful state of mutual thanks, conscious gratitude and ecstasy, instead of being lost in an unconscious union, according to Schopenhauer and Wagner: *unbewusst—grösste Lust* ("unconscious—greatest pleasure").

Compared with the new religions, especially those with an

Eastern influence, with their programs of I-am-you (meaning I as well as you will become *id*), personal love seeks the discrete togetherness of a mutual I-am-yours. In other words, the other person is not merely an entrancing, delightful gift which fulfills the partner, but at the same time the other person is also a responsibility who demands self-realization and fulfillment. The partners must neither devour nor allow themselves to be devoured but rather accept and receive the other person, and accept from her/him the gifts s/he offers and through which s/he offers her/himself.

It is true that a lover does not cling to her/his own person, as if s/he were "a thing to be grasped" (Phil. 2:6); but neither does s/he relinquish her/himself (perhaps in order not to have to give her/himself). On the contrary, s/he is attached to the possibility of letting-go, and therefore preserves the duality of I and You for the sake of the unity of love and togetherness.

This discernment between Who and What (Giver/Gift) and between I and Thou (Recipient/Giver) is the task of modesty.[9] It does not cover up anything shameful, but it preserves a precious object (its violation leads to shame!). Modesty preserves the distinction not as a kind of reservation but as a gift: modesty preserves its being given and accepted as precious. From the point of view of love, modesty means respecting the partner's mystery. And mystery does not mean riddle, although many think they should appear thus. A riddle is a torment, as long as it is not revealed, and becomes uninteresting after its revelation; a mystery, however, is something that attracts and that makes one feel at home. The all-encompassing, by definition, cannot be grasped, not because it does not wish to be grasped, but precisely because it completely and generously engulfs everything.

This is the only way in which freedom can truly be free (instead of relinquishing itself in total dependency). It gives itself

9. Jörg Splett, "Prüfstein Diskretion," in *Lernziel Menschlichkeit: Philosophische Grundperspektive*, 2d ed. (Frankfurt am Main: Verlag J. Knecht, 1981).

freely, that is, in full sovereignty: freedom decides to offer itself freely. Of course this includes the possibility of disagreeing, which is probably the first thing that comes to mind in connection with the term "freedom." But in essence it means that even one's agreement is confirmed (instead of being mere acquiescence). Freedom is therefore characterized by an inner duality; it "must" confirm its own agreement: its decision means that it has promised to give itself to someone. And active compliance with this promise is only possible if it is done freely: in faithfulness, as the identity of freedom in time.

That is why freedom requires trust; it needs faith, not only in relation to its promise as a "pledge" but also for the fulfillment of the promise. The reason is that freedom can only give itself in this way, that is, by giving *something* (other than itself). In other words the giving of oneself totally, without reservation, can never objectively be grasped. One can only grasp the gift but not the act of giving and its accompanying freedom, not its love and its essence. To use an image: one can only have a source of water by letting the water flow into one's hand; the only thing one can hold in the hand is a puddle. Mistrust (or "little faith"), however, interprets this incomprehensible situation as a reservation, and, in view of our daily reality, there are good reasons to do so. We may even speak about the need for mistrusting ourselves: does the "loving person" really know the extent of her/his love and its purity? And even if s/he should have a "clean conscience": how can s/he know it is not merely her/his "thick skin"?[10]

What "proofs of love" could possibly remove the risk of belief? Should we therefore not believe at all, or, at any rate, only

10. So too in a similar manner, when the prophet Nathan tells him the story of the rich man and the poor man, King David clearly had a good conscience, right up to the lightning-call: "You are the Man!" (2 Sam. 12:7). The word "incomprehensible" can also mean "unbearable" in German. Thus the diary entry of Max Frisch acquires its full meaning: ". . . the person one loves is incomprehensible—only love therefore can bear him." *Gesammelte Werke in zeitlicher Folge* (Frankfurt am Main: Suhrkamp, 1976), 2:369.

with a "hypothetical belief"? It becomes apparent here how the encounter with the Other, the stranger, forces the self to go out of him/herself. And the stranger *kat'exochen* is the person of the opposite gender, since men and women clearly speak different languages. Unlike the programs advocating oneness, androgyneity, and the "self satisfied person," here sexuality is understood as a special call to leave familiar ground behind and venture into unfamiliar territory.

Opening up to the Wholly (=Non) Other

If this existential meeting is a trusting and thankful togetherness of man and woman, it can open up a relationship that goes beyond the two individuals. Whither? For thousands of years the answer would be: to the child, or rather to procreation, whose force and urge the two individuals are serving. But here we were referring not merely to the individual and vital aspects but to the personal aspects of the relationship.

It comes as no surprise that, since time immemorial, the overwhelming experience of the Other has been a preferred means of initiation into the mysteries of the Wholly-Other. The Epiphany of one is so different that it would be better to follow Nicolas of Cusa in calling it the *Non-Other.* In this way sexual and marital experience as such became sacred, and sexuality was deified, or rather, idolized. The prophets of Israel fought these phenomena in a never-ending struggle. Even today such "Baalisation" can be found in art and literature, sometimes even in theology.

On the other hand, this fascination also helps to explain the rejection and demonization of sexuality in the history of Christianity; especially for Christianity because it is only here that woman and man have become conscious of being a person. After all, the profanation of sexuality can easily turn into demonization. Sexuality is not just one of many needs like hunger or thirst, for example; rather, it commits the individual in a far more personal manner and pushes her/him dramatically beyond her/his own limits; and unless her/his nature as a person and her/his personal dignity are recognized and treated with respect, sexuality can use and abuse her/him.

Man and woman are not meant to form a superhuman—original or utopian—unit into which they would simply merge. Neither are they merely helpmates, focusing on each other or functioning for each other. No one can be all things to another person, however congruent the two may be. This is a fact so basic that not even children could close this gap.

Nevertheless it would be unjust—and in view of the real experience of small and great joys, strangely "abstract"—to regard Sexus/Eros simply as a misfortune or a serious tragedy. Again and again people are able to marvel at the way they are given to one another. Given by whom?

Enter the Third party. This may be acknowledged in different ways: In the thankfully raised eyes after the mutual experience of bliss, as an instance of justice and truth and a guarantor of dignity in disagreements, as an instance to whom protest and complaints may be addressed when suffering and injustice are experienced; as a support in the efforts of the individual and the couple, as a hope for the fulfillment of a "pledge" (since the quintessence of joy is the promise of happiness to come).

This, however, leads us to another problem. How can one do justice both to a "temporal" and an "eternal Thou"? Not by dividing one's heart since the partners both want it undivided.[11] Perhaps by going through the Other and beyond her/him to God.[12] Would not then greater, truly human, love require one to renounce God for the sake of the partner?

11. "Two eyes has the soul: one is looking into the world, the other one into eternity." Angelus Silesius, *Sämtliche Poetische Werke,* 2d ed. (Munich: Allgemeine Verlagsanstalt, 1924), 3:131. And as Augustine observed, "When both eyes are open, the right one cannot look at something which the left one does not see." In *1 Ep. Joh.,* VI 10.

12. Thomas Aquinas concerning Paulus's liking of Philemon: "To delight

The liberating answer was given as early as the twelfth century by Richard of St.Victor,[13] by showing that the love between only two beings is lacking in true *condilectio* (oneness). Either the two beings move in opposite directions, each one towards the other, without *condilectio*, or they merge into each other (the I into the Thou, the Thou into the I, or both in one or in a "between") without *condilectio*. But if we look at it from the point of view of magnanimous generosity (which constitutes not only the beginning but also the starting-point and the basis for our considerations here), we may recognize that the I-Thou needs the joint We in relation to a Third one in order to become perfect.

I would first like to describe the phenomenon in terms of an abstract structural formula: I can only become a conscious I through an I-Thou relationship. Someone (whom I call Thou) calls me Thou. "We" is proportionately more complicated. Two are facing each other as I and Thou; two speak to each other about a Third one—and only thus they can become "We." If there were only two, it would never occur to them to form the word "we" in addition to "I" and "you." From speaking about the Third one, they go on to address Him jointly. The I-Thou became known thanks to Martin Buber; however, he only contrasts it with an *I-id*, not a We-Him, unfortunately.[14]

We must now inject some dynamic breath into the structural framework of the formula. For in this triangular set-up *each one* is the Third one in a twosome, serving as the "friend of the bridegroom" (Jn. 3:29) in their common interest, and at the same time each one celebrates her/his own wedding, thus joined with her/his Thou even better able to love the respec-

---

in one's friend *(frui)* he does not see as an end, but as a means *(tamquam medio)" STh* I–II, 3 ad 1.

13. For a more extensive explication than the one found in note 2, see Jörg Splett, *Freiheits-Erfahrung: Vergegenwärtigungen christlicher Anthropo-theologie* (Frankfurt am Main: Knecht, 1986), chap. 4–6, IV: Trinitarischer Sinn-Raum.

14. Further moments of differentiation follow out of the being-for-both of the third and his I-Them-opposite.

tive Third one. In this manner neither one is a means to an end, but each one is an intercessor and a source as well as a target of generosity.[15]

Is this too far-fetched? Is it completely "contra-factual"? Does it not at least serve to explain why we are suffering from circumstances which are not the way they should be, and, on the other hand, does it not illuminate experiences of blissful togetherness, which, for the sake of truth, gratitude, or even the ethic of thought, we dare not keep quiet? The terms "thinking" and "thanking" are not only linked at the etymological level (in German); thanklessness also denotes thoughtlessness and, *vice versa*, because truth is "concrete."[16]

Nobody expects all problems to be solved and all questions to be answered at this time.[17] But perhaps it is now possible to

15. Thus the basic figure of personal *condilectio* is not a "seamless" two in one, but a freely-giving tri-unity, and this also explains how two beings, whose "we" unites them in view of God, can cope with a child—or another "fourth" party—as a center of a new triangular relationship, without it completely upsetting their previous life pattern. This gives us, as already stated, the basic understanding of Love as an answer instead of a striving. Otherwise the relationship comes with the third in a rivalry of imitation, which allows, according to René Girard, murder as the roots of our culture. See especially *La violence et le sacré* (Paris: B. Grasset, 1972).

16. This also sheds some light on the celibate way of life and on the interrelationship of the two Christian life-projects. The "threesome" will be arranged in two basic "modes": maritally, in *condilectio* with God (as each of the two having her/his mysterious relationship with God and, at the same time, full of tender loving care for the partner), or through celibacy (since every Christian stands before God in the company of her/his fellow Christians) together with God for those who are sent by Him. Thus one state reflects the other and highlights in the other's example what the other state does not show. The "distant" and "virginal" component of marriage is revealed through the state of "passion for God." See Johannes Bours and Franz Kamphaus. *Leidenschaft für Gott: Ehelosigkeit, Armut, Keuschheit* (Freiburg: Herder, 1981). The component of "surrender" (instead of self-preservation) of the state of the evangelical vows is magnified through the sacramentality of the marriage. The remaining hierarchical difference between the two states (not the persons in them) appears to me in the fact, that, if there should be no resurrection after all, it is not the married Christians who "will be worse off than all others" (I Cor. 15:19).

17. One might even consider something that is not due to the sacramental

see that the human condition, as such, does not basically and unavoidably need to be seen as absurd and tragic, an affirmation which can be heard in our countries and which is especially preached as the "noble truth" by the powerful alternative to the three Abrahamic religions. The central mystery of our faith, which is unfortunately seldom considered and proclaimed—namely, the self-revelation of the triune God—also gives, with "all things added" (Mt. 6:33), a reply to our paradoxical desire for a fulfillment in which "One *and* Two are behind us."[18]

---

nature of marriage (all sacraments have to do with the Life, Death, and Resurrection of Jesus Christ): namely that the tension between absoluteness and multiple conditionality, pain and suffering ("I can bear you"), and even death belong to marriage, not only partially, but essentially. Moreover, at the end (without explanation, differentiation, the effort at averting misunderstanding and misuse, this will inevitably seem unacceptable), pain, suffering, and death are not mere shadows that cannot be cast off, but, although reluctantly, they are awaited. See Jörg Splett, "Schwachheit als Gnade und Wohltat des Schmerzes," in *Spiel-Ernst: Anstösse christlicher Philosophie* (Frankfurt am Main: Verlag J. Knecht, 1993).

18. Hans Urs von Balthasar, *Das Weizenkorn*, 8th ed. (Einsiedeln, Switz.: Johannes Verlag, 1958), 15.

Michel Rouche

3 THE MANY CHANGES IN THE CONCEPT OF CHRISTIAN MARRIAGE AND THE FAMILY THROUGHOUT HISTORY

The original meaning of the word "family" has little in common with its current usage—to describe children grouped around a father and mother. It was used to describe any group of people related by blood, of the same origin, carrying out the same activities and performing the same functions. Christianity strove to bring about change in these extended communities of blood relations, slaves and servants, by transforming them from within. Thus the structure of the family was changed in several stages; from the civil contract to polygamy, the Christian couple, the rejection of the indissoluble couple, and finally, the temporary couple.

For the Romans, conquerors of many alien peoples, marriage was a binding contract in which power was held by the husband. Everyone was bound to marry. While this civic obligation was seen as a bitter duty by some, it was nevertheless considered indispensable. Towards the year 100 B.C. a censor declared: "We all know that marriage is a headache, but marry we must, it is our civic duty." It was essential for the continued health of the community, and for this reason, the husband had unlimited authority over his wife and children, as well as the slaves, clients, etc., all those who made up his family. His wife, the mother figure, was to be absolutely pure, above all base sexual desire, and she was to produce legitimate offspring. For the Romans, women were little more than children, beings of unpredictable whims and fancies to be humored and pandered to for the sake of their dowry, which guaranteed their material independence. If a woman's husband was away from home, for example, working as an official in the provinces, she might take it into her head to divorce him *in absentia*. He might well find the house empty upon his return home. By the early years of the Roman Empire, the common people had adopted the practice of divorce by simple consent or by unilateral decision. In Juvenal's writings we see a woman of the people consulting a soothsayer to determine whether or not she should leave her innkeeper husband for a second-hand clothes dealer. Furthermore, marriage was monogamous in theory only, since there were always slave mistresses, favorites, and concubines.

From the second century A.D. opposition had arisen against this disordered state of affairs, from religion as well as from pagan philosophy, in the form of puritanical Stoicism. To counter the rise in Oriental cults deifying sex, the new thinking stressed that the mother should devote herself exclusively to her child. Concubinage was tolerated for those women who could not get married, and concubernal relationships were tolerated to satisfy sexual needs.

Because the female libido was held to be dangerous, the Stoics advised a marriage of friendship for couples in conflict, such as the widow whose lover was trying to extort a will or the master whose slave concubine demanded that he free their son. Although Ovid maintained that women were more faithful than men, the fear of female passion soon spread.

With Musonius, Rufus, Seneca, and Plutarch, the idea of a

relationship based on reason and friendship gained popularity. It held that women were to love and be loved only as friends and companions, as passionate love was degrading, even within marriage. Love was shameful enslavement, and sexuality the root of all danger. The only acceptable models for male-female relationships were those of Philemon and Baucis, or Paetus and Caecina. Caecina, doomed to commit suicide with her husband, does not hesitate to plunge the knife into her chest, draw it out, and hand it to her husband, saying "Here, take it, Paetus, it does not hurt!" Such is the ideal of the Stoical woman, free of all passion, the virago or woman who could behave just like a man. In reality, these Stoical couples, starting with Marcus Aurelius and Faustina, only put up an appearance of living together in happiness and harmony. Every time the Romans minted a new coin with the inscription *Concordia Augustorum,* they would say "and look, these two have just been fighting again." Despite the Stoical philosophy the number of separations continued to grow, and more and more people chose to live in concubinage for social, legal, and psychological reasons. Since the Roman marriage was merely a contract between equal partners of the same rank, which could be ended unilaterally, living together seemed a far more practical alternative. The young St. Augustine lived for fourteen years with a woman, but his mother forced him to abandon his mate when she found a young woman of suitable rank for her son to marry.

This practice explains why the Christian Church has such difficulty in dealing with this situation. From before the coming of the barbarians, the Church had sought to lay the basis for marriage on freedom of choice. In doing so, it adopted an adage from Roman law, "Marriage is based on consent." It was especially important that women be free to give their consent and not find themselves married as early as the age of twelve. By the fourth century A.D. the average age for a Roman woman to be married was eighteen to twenty. But this small amount of progress was quickly wiped out when the Germanic tribes settled in the West.

Indeed, the arrival of the barbarians meant the return in strength of the extended, clan-like or tribal family. The clan was made up of women, children, and relations up to six times removed and centered around the chief. Even warriors serving the Chief were included in the clan. The Chief was the holder of the *Mund* or power of protection over the weak—the women and children. On giving his daughter up for marriage, he transmitted the *Mund* to his son-in-law. It was indispensable that the bride was virgin. It was by virtue of her virginity that she received the *Morgengabe,* or literally "morning gift," on the morning of her wedding. The *Morgengabe* was a dower made up of her husband's belongings and this, along with her dowry, guaranteed her material independence. If she committed adultery she would be hanged or burned at the stake. If the official, or first wife, had no children, the husband could take second wives of lower rank, called *Friedelehen,* or guarantors of harmony. They were free concubines or slaves. Furthermore, in order to preserve alliances between related clans, these unions were very often endogamic. In short, these marriages were merely sexual and financial arrangements aimed at strengthening the community. In view of the union with one's relatives, alliances by blood were always considered the strongest. Love had no part in such arrangements. Indeed love was seen as subversive and destructive, since it could lead to adultery and hence to mortal danger. The prototype of this could be seen in the story of Tristan and Isolde who were bound together by a love potion that they had both drunk but that had not been intended for them. Indeed, all Germanic societies firmly believed that women were capable of concocting aphrodisiacs and potions to provoke abortions and even refrigerants.

The Church therefore had a long struggle to gain acceptance for its doctrine of indissoluble and monogamous marriage. Its main battle from 571 to 1215 A.D. was against consanguinity that was prohibited, starting with consanguinity to the third and then up to the sixth degree. Polygamy slowly disappeared after the reign of Charlemagne; Louis the Pious was the first king to have only one wife at the time. As slavery slowly declined, monogamy became more widespread, despite the fact that some highly placed people murdered their wives so that they could remarry soon after. In 869 the Church excommunicated Lothair II, King of Lorraine, who wanted to separate from his wife Teutberge because she was unable to have children. Following the reverberations caused by this affair, repudiation of a wife on the grounds of sterility also began to decline.

On a pedagogical level, the Church authorities sought to create a new language of love to remove the stigma attached to the word "love". Pope Innocent I introduced the expression *dilectio* for "tender love." In 824, Jonas, Bishop of Orléans, used the term *caritas conjugalis* meaning "conjugal love." In short, although the religious wedding ceremony existed but was still not widely practiced, the idea of a marriage founded on the love of Christ had already begun to win acceptance.

The classical Middle Ages saw the triumph of the nuclear, exogamous Christian marriage. From the eleventh to the thirteenth century, the influence of lineage in the choice of marriage partners declined, except within the nobility. However, parents continued to have an important say in the choice of partners. Women were relatively well protected by customary law as far as their property was concerned. The large-scale clearing and dividing of land helped peasants to acquire a measure of economic autonomy, and, as a result of this autonomy, a wife became mistress of the mutual household. From then on, a sentence first used by St. Augustine and repeated by Isidore of Seville in the sixth century, Hugh of St. Victor in the twelfth, and Vincent of Beauvais in the thirteenth century—"A woman is neither mistress nor servant but a companion"—finally became a reality. In his *Libri Sententiarum,* which was a handbook for future priests up to the time of the Renaissance,

Peter Lombard stresses the fact that women are superior to men in their capacity to love. Through the influence of the monks, especially of St. Bernard of Clairvaux, all those who, like him, contributed commentaries on the *Song of Songs,* Christ's love for the Church is expressed in terms of earthly love. In accounts of the life of Mathilda, her role as a mother is placed on the same level of importance as that of consecrated celibacy. This balance between spiritual and earthly love lasted until the end of the thirteenth century thanks to Franciscan spirituality and, it held its own despite the revival of pagan concepts of love in the form of courtly love, despite the rejection of sexuality by the Cathars, and finally, even despite bawdy bourgeois literature.

With the crisis of Medieval civilization came one of the first setbacks to the Christian concept of marriage. A strong current of misogyny developed in literature. An example of this was Jean de Meun's *Roman de la Rose.* The return of Roman law also brought about a decline in the status of women. But the primary new development was the trend towards marrying later in age, thereby extending the adolescent years. For some, it became impossible to remain chaste while awaiting marriage. "One cannot go against the call of nature" was the reason adduced by the judges for acquitting men of rape. The town councils, whether seeking to avoid misadventures to married women or to discourage the development of male homosexuality, often chose to open brothels. With the return to popularity of the writers of Antiquity, this misogynist trend was accompanied by the belief that one's sexual instinct cannot be repressed and that celibacy is impossible. Finally, the return of prosperity in the time of Renaissance brought with it a desire for sensual pleasure. The criticism of Christian marriage found its intellectual justification in the ideas of Luther.

Luther rejected the idea that the union of Christ and the Church was a symbol for Christian marriage. For him it was not a symbol but rather a mere allegory. By detracting importance from the sacrament of marriage, Luther robs woman of her spiritual fecundity. Sexuality is therefore cut off from divine love and finds itself brought to a human dimension. It is true that this return to pagan humanism did initially restore to the Protestant concept of marriage a balance and *joie de vivre* that it had lost. It is nonetheless true that from the beginning of the seventeenth century this same pagan humanism also led to the resurgence of puritanism, which in its turn, three generations later, corrupted Catholicism.

In the face of this radical challenge, the Catholic Church had refused the predominance of historical, finite time over the eternal duration of Christian marriage. The Council of Trent (1545–1563) reaffirmed the idea of the spiritual fecundity of consecrated celibacy and of marriage. For the first time in a conciliar text, the sacrament of marriage is seen in an optimistic light. The reasons for marriage are instinct, mutual support, children and sometimes, even passion. The human and divine dimensions are indivisible. This doctrine, which became known as devote humanism, was extremely successful wherever it was applied immediately after the Council of Trent. The works of Francis of Sales are directed at a new type of Christian couple for whom procreation is not the sole reason for marriage. It considers that living together, mutual pleasure, prayer, and the teaching of the Christian faith to their children are all equally important. A new relationship is established within the couple. The man and woman are equal, even though the decision-making role is still reserved for the man. Statistical studies of the time show us that public officials now systematically take the side of women over brutal spouses (the Cambrai case is an example).

But in the Kingdom of France the effects of the Tridentine Reforms made themselves felt very slowly. The decrees were published surreptitiously in 1615, fifty-two years later. The nobility, with the King as its natural protector, opposed freedom of consent for couples as stipulated by the Council. In 1556 the Blois decree stated that for all marriages, the parents' consent was indispensable. In 1560 another decree prohibited the remarriage of widows, thereby preventing their property from going to the family of their second husband. The Church, for its part, had always allowed the remarriage of widows, since the sacrament of marriage is the only one in which the bodies of the spouses is the physical basis of the sacrament. Finally, another royal decree of 1730 likened marriage between two people who had attained their legal majority but who had not obtained their parents' consent to kidnapping and seduction. Up to the time of the Revolution, priests who agreed to marry couples according to the precepts of the Council of Trent were forced to appear before the royal tribunal. In this way the monarchic State robbed the Church of its jurisdiction over marriage. Furthermore, the success of the Tridentine Reform was overshadowed by the rise of Jansenism, the triumph of wild passion expressed in Racine's tragedies, and by the tragedy of marriage for the sake of convenience.

The beginning of the eighteenth century marked the start of a period of slow, yet irreversible and hitherto unknown, changes and events. These changes left the Church more than ever deprived of a voice, especially after Bossuet's condemnation of the mystic movement in 1694. This had broken the monopoly of the language of love which the Church had enjoyed up until then. This loss of the dominant voice lasted for more than a century.

One important development during the eighteenth century was the decrease in mortality and the rise in living standards. The fear of death, which had forced people to have many children, was now replaced by a fear of the over-abundance of life. Birth control by the method of *coitus interruptus* first appeared within the nobility and then spread to the peasants of Normandy and Aquitaine. The testimonies of 300 young women in Vexin show that they purposely chose to become pregnant by their lovers to force their parents to consent to their marriage.

Love no longer inspired fear. In the theater, Marivaux described the many ruses of love. In 1772 the Encyclopedia conceded that love between a married couple was normal. Nonetheless, among the nobility and bourgeoisie, love was still regarded as a wrong-headed impulse, and Madame Roland, who thought that on the day of one's wedding "love should be present," was regarded as a giddy romantic.

In actual fact, conjugal love had begun to acquire a good reputation. But what happens when love is absent because the couple has married for the sake of convenience? Here the influence of the intellectuals gives rise to a new model, free love. From 1733 to 1748, Voltaire was the lover of the Marchioness du Châtelet with the blessings of her overly obliging husband. Then, when "his pistol no longer fired," as he put it, he stepped aside for a younger and more vigorous man, Saint-Lambert. This latter had the bad taste to make the Marchioness pregnant, and she died in childbirth in 1749. This earned for Saint-Lambert (and this may come as a surprise for some) the wrathful condemnation of Voltaire. However, Voltaire soon found consolation in the person of Madame Denis, his niece who was able to arouse in him an ardor and a passion that he had thought long extinguished. In short the trio soon passed to the quatuor, which in its turn was superseded by the quintet. Small wonder, then, that for the enthusiasts of the Century of the Lights, the eighteenth century also marked the highest peak of excellence in chamber music. However, another rival model had appeared. Its exponent was Rousseau, who was afraid of sex and so chose a simple-minded and submissive mistress. In *La Nouvelle Heloïse* he favors a marriage where the wife is content to accept the "gentle consolation of virtue." In this echo of Seneca, we can see that "the breakdown of morals," to use the expression of the period, had come about long before the Revolution.

This breakdown in morals appeared to reach the common people during the years 1750–1760. Marital fidelity, which up

until then had been the expectation and the norm, fell abrupt-
ly away. The number of illegitimate births rose by 10%, especially in the towns. Sexual perversion now appeared in the writings of the Marquis de Sade and, with its misleading moralistic
title, in Choderlos de Laclos' *Liaisons Dangereuses.* But it was a
poet and priest, Delille, who for the first time used the word
"couple" to describe a pair of lovers. Up until then, the word
had been used exclusively for animals.

The French Revolution pushed the logic of freedom in love
to its very limit. Considering any perpetual alliance to be an at-
tack on freedom, it did away with perpetual vows and introduced civil marriage and divorce by mutual consent. In 1795
the number of divorces outstripped the number of marriages.
The results were so devastating that the ideologues, with Napo-
leon's agreement, amended the Civil Code so that the only
grounds for divorce was adultery—adultery by the wife, natu-
rally. According to Merlin de Douai, former Parliamentary
deputy, "Women are by nature incapable of governing, men
have a natural superiority over them!" The couple and the family are here placed under the authority of the head of the family. Patrimony takes precedence over mutual affection. Following on all of this, the abolition of divorce in 1826 went unno-
ticed. Marriage was once more a social contract in which the
Church did not figure.

Unlike the eighteenth century with its revolutionary up-
heavals, the nineteenth century was marked by order, be it
moral or secular. Catholicism found itself pitted against ratio-
nalism, although they shared a common puritanical and pes-
simistic vision of sexuality and agreed on the central role of the
mother. Despite this the Church embarked upon fresh efforts
to bring Christianity back into marriage. To this end between
1840 and 1880, the Church chose to ally itself with romanti-
cism, heightened by a strict ultramontane piety. Among the
common people, this new trend found its expression in the
style of Saint-Sulpice, whereas among the elite it was Balzac's

Mémoires de deux jeunes mariées or the violent passion of Franz Liszt for Marie Agoult. But it was a passion that was finally turned again towards the Church. So effective was this romantic model of the one and only true love that by the end of the century, the practice of concubinage had disappeared among the working classes.

Little by little, what had been a luxury reserved for the rich had spread to the people: a cheap photograph of the loved one made it possible to keep on hand the imagistic equivalent of the masterpiece of the young bride that adorned the homes of the rich. This democratization of love made it possible to choose one's partner, while the number of marriages of convenience decreased with the disappearance of the dowry.

But at the same time, the radical Voltairian bourgeoisie, satisfied that a conservative and moralistic Church had effectively reined in their wives within the strictures of marital fidelity, militated in favor of free love. The life of Guy de Maupassant is an eloquent example of this. Furthermore, they favored a revocable contract which would allow them to remarry as they pleased. In 1884 the Naquet Law allowed one to obtain a divorce by establishing proof of guilt. Thus started the practice whereby a detective inspector would stand in a room in the wan light of dawn, recording an adultery by the evidence of dishevelled beds and sleep-creased bodies. If one's wife was virtuous and therefore not easily got rid of, there remained a simple solution: that of the kept woman in an apartment who slept all week long and engaged in frenzied house-cleaning as Saturday approached. The Feydeau comedies effectively illustrate this infernal triangle of husband, wife, and lover. This is a system of moral double standards with one marriage out of fifty ending in divorce. The marriage of the parents of Winston Churchill, two unrestrained libertines, sharply contrasts with the rigorous austerity of their son's marriage.

This fragile balance was shattered by the First World War. There was greater instability with the extremely high percentage of male mortality and the overwhelming number of war widows, who, as Colette put it, "want a man as surely as they are scalded by cold water." The falling off in religious practice by women further exacerbated an already unstable situation. However, this deterioration was concealed by the fact that towards 1930, female life expectancy was fifty years as opposed to forty-eight years for men. Furthermore, from 1930 to 1960 there was a new wave of Christianization of marriage, with the birth of marital spirituality movements. The *Equipes de Notre-Dame* are an example of these. The Encyclical *Casti Connubii* of 1930 was very well received.

But all of this progress peaked after the Second World War. The return home of prisoners of war was not without surprises, as far as fidelity was concerned. By 1959, the divorce rate had risen to one in every nine marriages. Human life expectancy increased steadily, to eighty-one years for women and seventy-eight for men. Now, when people get married, they could expect to be together for some fifty years. With the prosperity of the Glorious Thirties came a new model, epitomized by the relationship of Jean-Paul Sartre and Simone de Beauvoir. After free love, it was now the freedom of the individual and the pact of honesty. It was tell all, reveal all, even mutual infidelities. Even Simone de Beauvoir was struck by this insidious justification of male infidelity; she expressed surprise at the hurt she suffered: "To think I was so taken in." Their immense influence was especially strong after the events of May 1968 in France. The laws of 1975 authorizing divorce by mutual consent and the 1976 law legalizing abortion in France led to a rejection of commitment. The number of marriages fell from 400,000 per year to 300,000. At the same time there was an increase in the number of couples living together, one-parent families and matri-focal units. All of these factors, together with the exaggerated importance of affection as the sole basis for a couple's relationship, helped push up the number of divorces in France to one out of every three marriages. Today, one child in three does not see or has never known his/her father.

The situation prevailing at the end of the twentieth century is only one of the many crises that have affected marriage throughout history. It merely goes to prove that progress cannot be reached without painful changes, since freedom must fight against licentiousness. Each stage of progress is followed by a period of crises. New progress is already in the making. Because it is a conflict between two opposing concepts of love and marriage; one of which only seeks to remain a part of history, while the other feels the call of eternity.

Ladislas Örsy, S.J.

4 MARRIED PERSONS: GOD'S CHOSEN PEOPLE

The title of this inquiry is really an affirmation: according to God's eternal design, within the Christian church, some persons have been chosen to be consecrated for a particular state of life, married life, that is, and thus contribute to the building of his kingdom.[1] This

1. In order to understand and appreciate the nature and the content of this essay, its literary genre ought to be explained and its position in the theological literature determined.

Theology can be done at different levels. A researcher may wish to report on all the data that he found and used: the result is usually a highly technical study attractive for specialists only. Or, an inquirer may give an account of the critical steps that he has taken in order to reach his conclusions: such work again is likely to have a limited appeal.

The purpose of this present essay is to communicate significant conclusions reached through study and reflection, but not the details of research which have led to them. Information concerning historical data and doctrinal positions with extensive bibliographical references can be found in the author's works *Marriage in Canon Law* (Wilmington, Del.: Glazier, 1986) and *Theology and Canon Law* (Collegeville, Minn.: Liturgical Press, 1992).

Persons familiar with the field will know that behind the seeming simplicity of several conclusions there are problems of great complexity. Although for some foundational issues we have been given signifi-

choice becomes definitive and manifest in the sacramental event of matrimony, which in its turn ought to be a source of life for the couple and for the Christian community as a whole.[2] The purpose of our inquiry is to seek and reach a better understanding of this mystery and to take a critical look at the practicalities surrounding it.

The sacred event of matrimony could be described also as a drama in the original, classical sense of the term: a deed, an action, performed on a scene, where the participants are often moved by hidden forces and energies.[3] Here, as in all sacraments, the leading actors who initiate and carry the movement of the play are the divine persons. They remain invisible to our bodily eyes: they can be seen with the eyes of faith only. The

---

cant clarifications by Vatican Council II, much remains to be explored. For examples of outstanding problems see "Problem Areas and Disputed Questions," in *Marriage in Canon Law*, 260–94.

2. I use the term "chosen" in a sense similar to that in Acts 9:15: "for he [Paul] is an instrument whom I have chosen," (also Act 1, 2:24) signifies an election for a purpose. The aim is to stress God's initiative. There is a powerful message in this seemingly simple terminology—namely, in the Christian dispensation there are different, grace-filled gifts: marriage is one of them; another is to remain unmarried for the sake of the Kingdom. This approach breaks away from a theory that presented married life as "less-than-perfect," and religious life as the "perfect state of life." How much that theory penetrated the mentality of people can be judged from the common way of speaking: "to have a vocation" is regularly understood as to have a call to priesthood or to religious life. If that is true, married persons "do not have a vocation"—a patently absurd assertion. Jesus certainly honored the vocation of the bride and bridegroom of Cana! "To be chosen" in this case is equivalent to "being called"; God cannot address a personal call to someone without selecting, that is, choosing him or her for a specific task. Married persons, altogether, are indeed a "people" chosen for a task in the Kingdom.

3. To see a sacrament as a drama brings home immediately the dynamic character of the mystery; from the start, this understanding excludes any definition of a sacrament that would present it as a static structure. This approach is more contemplative than analytical, more intuitive than conceptual. It has its roots in the "existential" character of patristic theology; it has some affinity with the writings of modern Orthodox theologians. In the West, in recent times, Hans Urs von Balthasar used it: in his writings he presented the events of our redemption as a divine play, *theo-drama*.

other players are the human persons: a man and a woman seeking a union. In them, the plan of God unfolds. The scene is "eternity in time." The source of hidden forces and energies comes from grace and nature. There is also a chorus, as it befits a true drama: it is the larger Christian community that assists in preparing the play; it is present at the celebration and provides support afterwards.

Since God is the principal actor in this drama, the prime questions are about *him:* how he deals with his children when he calls them to marry, as he joins them in marriage, and while he holds them together in a life-long partnership. Thus, let us ask: first, what are God's thoughts (as revealed) concerning marriage? second, what is he doing when a man and a woman promise life-long fidelity to each other? third, how is he supporting them in their married life? In all these questions faith seeks understanding. In the responses a cohesive doctrine should emerge.

Living faith, however, is never content with knowledge alone: it seeks action. Our perception of God's thoughts and deeds ought to become a wellspring for our operations: without such integration there is no Christian life. We must, therefore, raise a fourth question: what practical consequences flow from the Christian doctrine of marriage—in the fields of spirituality, liturgy, and canon law?[4]

---

4. The connecting link between theory and practice, or between vision and action, is in the perception of values. Christian mysteries reveal moral values as well; the desire for perfection prompts for the appropriation of those values. Thus, vision generates action: moral decisions flow from doctrinal knowledge in a harmonious sequence. The energy feeding this movement comes from the dynamics of the human spirit lifted up into the realm of the "new creation" by God's own spirit.

The inspiration for this wholesome explanation comes from the philosophy of Joseph Maréchal of Louvain who built his epistemology (and metaphysics) on the innate *dynamisme de l'intelligence,* which can be (and has been) broadened into the discovery of the dynamism of the human spirit and of divine grace. Karl Rahner, Johannes B. Lotz, Joseph de Finance, Bernard Lonergan—to name only a few—expanded vastly the horizons opened up by Maréchal.

Faith Seeks Understanding

What are God's thoughts about marriage?

Let us begin with the creation story: "So God created humankind in his image, in the image of God he created them; male and female he created them" (Gen. 1:27). In this sentence, there is a strong indication, to the point of an assertion, that the male and the female *together* reflect the image of God. They *together* possess a perfection that is not given to each one individually. Man and woman, in union, reveal the image, the personality, of their Creator better than one of them alone could do it.[5]

The next sequence in the biblical text confirms and carries this thought further: "God blessed them, and God said to them: 'Be fruitful and multiply, and fill the earth and subdue it . . .'" (Gen. 1:28). God commissions the couple, man and woman *together*, for a common task, which we could paraphrase in this way: "Although God rested on the seventh day, he left the work of creation unfinished. Henceforth he told them: 'You carry on with the task of populating the earth and with giving a purpose to the immense vital forces that it contains.'"

Another relevant story is that of God's covenant with Abraham and Sarah. Yes, with Sarah as well, because she is very much an active player throughout that saga. The covenant that God concluded with him was also binding toward her. *They* will have a son, and by *their* offspring "shall all the nations

---

5. An illustration might bring this point home. A chorus is much richer when male and female voices sing together than when it is confined to one gender. The difference in the voices and the resulting harmony bring a depth into the performance that otherwise would not be there, and the whole piece reveals the genius of the composer better.

An issue to be explored: if male and female *together* reveal (manifest) the image of God to a greater extent than either of them could do it alone, what is the significance of this for the theology of the sacrament of matrimony?

of the earth gain blessing for themselves" (Gen. 22:18). This story is relevant precisely because in it the pattern of God's covenant is revealed. (As we shall see, in the sacramental event of matrimony, God concludes a covenant with the couple.)

In the "drama" of Abraham, God is the initiator of all activity: he calls Abraham and Sarah; he promises a son to them (note that without Sarah the promise would be meaningless); he befriends them on their long journey; he sustains and defends them; and, in impeding the sacrifice of Isaac, he reveals his tenderness to them.

The responses of the couple throughout the events remain thoroughly human, so much so that we recognize ourselves in them! They believed and doubted: they set out on the journey, yet Sarah laughed skeptically at the promise of a child and said: "Shall I indeed bear a child, now that I am old?" (Gen. 18:13). They hoped and despaired: they cherished the image of the child to come, yet Abraham exclaimed, "You have given me no offspring . . . a slave . . . is to be my heir" (Gen. 15:3). God did not conclude a covenant with angels but with flesh and blood human beings (another anticipation of the sacramental covenant).

Further, there are telling passages in the New Testament concerning God's mind about marriage. The story of the wedding feast at Cana, where Jesus changed the water into wine, is a revealing one. There, "Jesus did this, the first of his signs, . . . and revealed his glory" (John 2:11). Although this narrative lends itself to many interpretations, it certainly conveys the idea that Jesus held marriage, or better, married persons, in high regard. In the beginning of his ministry, right after choosing of some of his apostles, he wanted to be present at a wedding. When it was brought to his attention that they had no wine, he gave them "good wine." Did Jesus remember how Yahweh was present at the encounter of the first man and woman and gave them the fruits of the earth? In any case, the gratuitous gift of this wine is a powerful symbol of God's tender care.[6]

The author of the Epistle to the Ephesians gives some far-reaching instructions as to what Christian marriage is and how it should be lived. It is a community of love and the head of it is Christ. The relations between the spouses ought to be modeled on the relation of Christ to his Church. He "gave himself up for her, in order to make her holy"; he "nourishes and tenderly cares" for her (cf. Eph. 5:21–33). The writer is effectively saying that each of the spouses should give up himself or herself for the other, as Christ did for the church. A life-long duty of giving, incumbent on each, with no restriction, no distinction, and no difference. Such love is beyond the capacity of any human being; it can come only from the Spirit. Marriages among pagans were never modeled on such excess of love.[7] Christian marriages belong to the order of the "new creation," where the saving action of God becomes incarnate in secular realities, although in the intention of God the saving action has an absolute priority.

These stories and exhortations convey to us a great deal about God's thoughts and ways. More could be found in the wealth of our revelation, but it is time to move to the second question.

What is God doing in the sacramental event of matrimony?

Our second question is about the sacramental event, in common language, the wedding ceremony: a central act in the drama. The physical scene is ordinarily that of a church building where the bride and the bridegroom meet, surrounded by

6. See the insightful pages by Xavier Léon-Dufour, "A Cana, les noces de Dieu avec Israel," in *Lecture de l'évangile selon Jean* (Paris: Seuil, 1988), 1:203–45.

7. This statement follows from a theological position not expounded here: there is a specifically distinct Christian way of living out the marriage covenant, as there is a specifically distinct Christian morality.

their families and friends, and where they are received by a priest. The visible action is simple: "they exchange vows"; that is, they promise life-long fidelity to each other. After that, the nuptial blessing follows, imparted by the priest.

Beyond the visible action, the play has an invisible dimension, perceived only by believers blessed with the "eyes of faith."[8] To grasp with some fullness this invisible dimension which animates the sacramental event, we have to pause for a moment and reflect on the general idea of sacrament; from there we shall move to the specific meaning of the sacrament of marriage.

A sacrament is not merely a sign that points to something else—such as a gift of grace. Nor is it just an "instrument that causes grace"—there is more to it. A sacrament stands on its own; it is God's own mighty deed and saving action expressed in symbols, which consist of words and gestures. Behind those symbols, divine and human persons meet, exchange gifts, and establish a new bond with each other.[9] This is what happens,

8. The expression "with the eyes of faith" receives a particular depth if it is understood according to the insights of Pierre Rousselot (1878– 1915): an infused capacity to perceive the words and deeds of God and their truth as well. For references see "Rousselot," in *LThK* 9.76.

9. This brief description of what a sacrament is represents the most incisive insight of Odo Casel (1886–1948): in a sacrament, the redeeming action of Christ is really present. His theory is a significant development over the classical scholastic approach that defined a sacrament as an efficacious sign of grace. For Aquinas himself, a sacrament was an "instrumental cause" of grace; grace that flowed from the original redeeming act of Christ. For Casel, there is no such mediation because there is a mysterious immediacy. In the symbol of the sacrament, the one permanent redeeming act of Christ is present. Our earthly space and time frame disappears: we are participating in the one and eternal saving act of God through the humanity of Christ and through the symbol of the sacrament. Casel showed the beauty and strength of his theory mainly in connection with the Eucharist; it clearly gives a rich new meaning to every sacrament. See Odo Casel, *The Mystery of Christian Worship* (London: DLT, 1962).

If baptism is an entrance "into the mystery," marriage is the entrance into a new status in the mysterious body of the elect. There is a promising source to enrich the theology of marriage: to see what inspiration can be found in the

but in a specific way, in the sacrament of marriage, behind those very ceremonies that we can see. The spouses (whether they think of it or not) are endowed with a mysterious power, given to them in their baptism. They partake in a "royal priesthood" (1 Pet. 2:9). They act from such a resource. Through their words and gestures, they consecrate each other to new tasks: to serve God by serving "and thus redeeming" each other and to cooperate with the Creator in bringing immortal persons into this mortal world. Manuals of theology affirm this by saying: "The spouses are the ministers of the sacrament." Truly, they are ministers of God, with a priestly power that was given them at their baptism.

The role of the ordained priest who witnesses the exchange of vows is ambivalent in the Western church: his presence is legally required, but theologically he is expendable. In the Eastern church his presence is essential: he is a *consecrator* in some real sense. He imposes a crown on them; this rite has an affinity with the ancient and sacred gesture of *xeirothesia*, the laying on of hands.

Be that as it may, in the West or in the East, the principal actor is our invisible God. He makes his covenant with the couple.[10] The nature of this covenant is the same that we find in his dealings with Abraham and Sarah and in his promises to Israel, his chosen people. It is a one-sided covenant. At the wedding, he pours out his Spirit on two human beings who are about to begin a life-long journey, and he promises to be with them and shelter them under the shadow of his wings.

God's covenant is not conditioned by the virtues of the bride

---

early mystagogies, especially that of St. Ambrose. For an orientation, see Enrico Mazza, *Mystagogy* (New York: Pueblo, 1989), especially the chapter on St. Ambrose, 14–44. Also the somewhat schematically written but original and thoughtful work of Lothar Lies, *Sakramententheologie* (Graz, Aust.: Styria, 1990).

10. Once the doctrine is accepted that God is the principal covenantor, and the consequences of this doctrine are pondered, it becomes clear that to conceive the sacrament on the pattern of a legal contract cannot do justice to the mystery.

and the bridegroom: he loves them and takes them as they are. They can be fragile like a bruised reed, or weak like a smoldering wick (cf. Matt. 12:20); God is strong and ready to give.[11] This covenant made by God is the central act of the drama.

Yet the wedding ceremony is only a beginning. After it, a new chapter opens, and this leads us to our third question.

How is God present to the couple—throughout their life?

Our focus now is on God's presence to the married couple.

He delights in them. To understand this, we should go back, once again, to the creation story in Genesis. God was delighted with his creatures, as the returning refrain testifies: "And God saw that it was good."[12] If such divine delight took place in the beginning, how much more it must be there today in these blessed times of our redemption. It makes sense to say that when God sees a man and woman, united by a sacred bond, intent to fulfill the task allotted to them, he indeed takes his delight in them. He finds his own image mirrored in them; he recognizes in them his partners in creation and *knows* that "it is good."

In particular, as God contemplates a man and woman intimately related to each other, as he looks at the children united to their parents, all held together by a bond of love, he must find in them a reflection of his own inner life where Father,

11. The brevity of this paragraph does not do justice to the weight of the doctrine contained therein: Christian marriage is not an unreachable ideal but an institution for weak and fragile human beings; in this, marriage shares the nature of baptism. It brings to the couple strength and redemption. God supports them as he supported Abraham and Sarah in their wanderings, who were equally weak and fragile persons.

At times, Christian marriage is presented as such a high ideal that people exclaim: who can live up to it?! Such a presentation may be well meant; it is false, nonetheless. The point is in God's firm commitment to his weak ones.

12. André Chouraqui in his *La Bible* renders it: *Elohîm voit tout ce qu'il avait fait, et voici: un bien intense* (Gen. 1:31), or earlier: *quel bien!* which is more an exclamation in the sense "God sees what he has made and is immensely pleased with it to the point of crying out: how good!" Remember that God *saw* his own creation the very first time!

Son, and Spirit are one and three—and where love knows no bounds.[13] He raises up a small church among his people. Traditionally, we believe and say that a Christian family is a Christian assembly, a small church, *ecclesia domestica*. Now, no one can bring a church, large or small, into existence except the Spirit of God—as no-one can say that "Jesus is the Lord" except in the Spirit.

Thus, this small church is "conceived in the Spirit" as the large one was on that day of Pentecost. The gifts granted to the large church, in due proportion, are present in the small one.[14] The Spirit of God animates it and sustains it, and the word of God is proclaimed in it and through it. Obligations follow: in the members there is a duty of openness to the inspirations of the Spirit and a duty to surrender to his voice. They must also receive and speak the word of God—and hand it over to others.[15]

Further, because it is an integral and organic part of the church universal, no such small church can exist in isolation. This integration is vital for both sides. The family receives the Word and the sacraments through the wider community, but that community receives its vitality from the families. Without them, it would not even exist.

The small domestic assembly is also in the service of the whole human family. This service it can do in myriads of ways,

13. The theology that inspired the paragraphs under the subtitle "He delights in them" excludes the position that would consider married life a "less-than-perfect" state of life.

14. An interesting study to be written: ecclesiology of the Christian family.

15. "To speak the word of God" raises the issue of domestic liturgy. This is not the place to elaborate on it, except to point out its power in preserving a faith community even among the most bitter persecutions. The survival of Jewish communities is a living proof of that: their traditional observance within the family of the Sabbath, Passover, and other festivities helped to keep their faith alive. In many places, Christians were an easier prey to the tyrants because their worship centered entirely on the parish. The destruction of the parish structure left them vulnerable without any liturgy and religious practice—with the ensuing damage to their faith and hope.

be it through quietly announcing the good news of the resurrection to those who are sitting in the shadow of death, or by demonstrating the compassion of God through charitable works, and so forth.

We believe that the church is sacrament: in it God meets our humanity. A Christian family is part of the whole: in it the drama of our redemption is enacted again.

Faith Seeks Action

How to move from doctrine to practice, from vision to action?

This is a broad question, and it opens up vast horizons. Broad as it is, we must raise it because it keeps us alert to the need for integration between understanding and action. In our on-going reflections, we progress to a point where we are like mountain climbers who have reached a peak and suddenly find themselves looking at a new and immense landscape—full of features to be explored.[16]

We cannot explore them thoroughly here and now. We can, however, notice some of the salient features and comment on them briefly. This I propose to do under three headings: spirituality, liturgy, and canon law.

Spirituality: doctrine and experience

Spirituality is a two-faceted reality: it is partly systematic theology, partly accumulated experience. John Henry Newman's distinction between shadows and images on the one hand, and truth—meaning existing reality—on the other hand, can be helpful in understanding this concept. Spirituality expressed in

---

16. In precise and somewhat philosophical terms, we are moving from the question "what is marriage" (a somewhat abstract issue) to the question "what should be done about the values that marriage represents" (a concrete issue throughout). The purpose of the first inquiry is to gather knowledge; the purpose of the second one is to move towards actions that can shape the existing world.

concepts and propositions remains in the realm of the shadows and images; spirituality that wells up from accumulated experience speaks of an encounter with God. The two mutually complete and balance each other; they are meant to blend together in a harmonious unity.

It follows that non-married persons can offer some valid reflections on marital spirituality, but they have no capacity to speak with authenticity about the personal encounter of married persons with their God.

This existential component of spirituality is never learned from the outside but is created from the inside. It is the fruit of the internal experience of the gentle grace of God and of the pondering of the word of God revealed and received. It is always personal: in a true sense, each person must have his or her own spirituality, although, obviously, the testimony of persons of similar vocation will converge strongly.

I do not wish to speak of marital spirituality as "lay spirituality" for two reasons. First, because by so speaking I would do injustice to St. Peter himself and to the other apostles—as well as to many bishops and presbyters in the early centuries who were married. Moreover, I would seem to suggest that the married clergy of our sister churches (whether in union with Rome or not) ought to live by "lay spirituality" alone. There is historical evidence that sacerdotal and marital spirituality can blend in harmony in the very same person.[17]

Second, "lay spirituality" is widely conceived today as confined to the task of sanctifying the secular world but having no part in the sacred activities of the church. Since in the Western church virtually all married persons are lay persons, it would follow that all married persons must be excluded from participating in any ecclesiastical operation that can be properly called sacred. In practice, this means the barring of the laity from participating in decision-making processes. Such an un-

17. This is in no way to detract from the charism of celibacy: "there are varieties of gifts, but the same Spirit" (1 Cor. 12:4).

derstanding of the "laity," current as it may be, is not in harmony with our traditions and has no sound theological basis. It divides the church into two sharply distinguished and separated groups: the clergy and the laity.[18]

Undoubtedly, Vatican Council II initiated a new doctrinal development in understanding the place and role of the non-ordained and of the married in the church, and this development is still going on. Significant practical changes are bound to follow.

Liturgy: the need for sacred symbols

There is an affinity between the sacrament of orders and the sacrament of matrimony. In each, a person is consecrated, "anointed by the Spirit" for a specific task in the community. In the case of orders, the mandate is for the service of the community at large; in the case of matrimony, for the building a small church, *ecclesia,* that is the family.

The principal sacramental symbol in ordination is the imposition (laying on) of the hands *(epithesis ton xeiron, xeirothesia)* with prayer. In the Western rite the sacramental symbol in marriage is the exchange of promises; there is little in the words and gestures to express the pouring out of the Spirit. In the Eastern church, as we have seen, the rite of marriage includes a gesture akin to the traditional imposition of the hands. It would be within the power (and the possibilities) of the Western church to build up a more expressive structure of symbols. Let us see how this could be done.

Initially, there should be a remembrance *(anamnesis)* of

---

18. Alexandre Faivre shows in his interesting studies that the laity as a separate class did not emerge until the middle of the third century. Before that time all members of the Christian community were thought of as *cleros,* chosen people, people set apart. See *Les laïcs aux origines de l'Eglise* (Paris: Le Centurion, 1984). For information concerning the contemporary situation of the laity in the church (Vatican Council II and its aftermath including the Bishops' Synod on Laity), see Jan Grootaers: *Le chantier reste ouvert: les laïcs dans l'Eglise et dans le monde* (Paris: Le Centurion, 1988).

God's saving deeds such as the creation story or the miracle at the wedding feast of Cana. A consecratory gesture could follow (imposition of the hands by the priest, anointing) with a prayer invoking the Spirit *(epiklesis)*. Then the bridegroom and the bride could exchange promises and thus conclude the covenant and establish the communion *(koinonia)* that God has initiated. At that point the rite of marriage could blend into that of the Eucharist where the couple becomes one with the risen Christ who offers them to the Father as a sacrifice of praise *(prosphora)*.

Although this sketch is all too brief, it indicates how a wholesome liturgical rite could go far beyond the idea of a pale contract and reflect the operations of the Trinity of the divine persons: the saving action of the Redeemer, the pouring out of the Spirit, and the sacrifice offered to the Father—to whom the whole creation is aspiring and returning.

Canon law: in the service of the mystery

Canon law is radically different from civil law. The purpose of civil law is to promote the temporal welfare of the citizens; the purpose of canon law is to provide a framework for God's saving deeds. Civil law should bring order and balance into the secular community; canon law should give an overriding scope to the gift of redemption. Civil law cannot go beyond the norms set by the human virtue of justice; canon law ought to be animated by the prodigality of divine charity. This is expressed in the Code of Canon Law itself: "The salvation of souls . . . is always the supreme law of the church" (canon 1752).[19]

19. This is not to take away the strictly legal character of some parts of canon law (for example, the one dealing with real property), but to give to all its parts a higher finality (the law of property not excepted). In traditional scholastic terms, this can be expressed also by saying that the theological virtue of charity ought to take precedence over the cardinal virtue of justice. No exception, ever, must be allowed to this rule because even the slightest exception would violate God's prime intention in creation itself. In making heaven and

Within canon law, the specific purpose of sacramental law is to assure that they who are qualified and well disposed have easy access to God in the mysteries. How does the canon law of marriage serve this purpose? The answer presents a mixed picture: we have a serviceable system but the legalities tend to overshadow the mystery. To understand the canon law of marriage, some historical information is necessary.

Until the tenth century, moral and legal issues concerning marriages were handled mostly by the local bishops or by those who had authority to absolve penitents, or occasionally, as in the case of princely families, by the popes. Although some decisions became increasingly normative, a cohesive body of marriage laws did not emerge until the twelfth century, when Roman law was re-discovered in the West.

Canonists, desirous of having a well-designed system for marriages, discovered it in the Roman law of contracts. Such a find was not without irony, because the classical lawyers of Rome (and of Byzantium, for that matter) never conceived of marriage as a contract. It never occurred to the ancient *iurisprudentes* to apply the rules created for commercial transactions to a *consortium cum affectu maritali*, to a partnership with marital affection. Canon lawyers did it, and have continued doing so ever since.[20]

Thus, marriage was defined as a contract, and many of the rules worked out for secular agreements were applied to a saving event. The primary end of the contract (so the law said) was the procreation of children; mutual help was ranked as a

---

earth, and in breathing the breath of life into man and woman, he already intended to grant his saving grace to all human beings.

20. Even among the best of the historians of Christian doctrine and sacramental practice, there is a fair amount of misunderstanding on this point. They think that because in ancient Rome no marriage was possible without the parties consenting, marriage must have been a consensual contract. In the mind of classical Roman lawyers, this was a *non sequitur;* as far as we know no *praetor* has granted an "action" *ex contractu maritali.* See Percy Ellwood Corbett, *The Roman Law of Marriage* (Aalen, Ger.: Scientia, 1979).

secondary end. One could say without exaggeration that the importance of love was lost in the shuffle.

This approach, where legalities indeed overshadowed the mystery, remained substantially unchanged until the Constitution of Vatican Council II, *Gaudium et Spes*. In its original Latin this insightful document speaks of marriage as *foedus;* the term is akin to the terms *fides* and *fidere,* carrying the meanings of faith and trust (GS, 47–52). The conventional translation of *foedus* into English is by the word "covenant." In this case the word assumes a special and solemn meaning, with a religious dimension and including certainly faith and trust.

The new Code of Canon Law was made in an effort to adjust the law to the mind of Vatican Council II. It defines marriage as covenant—then keeps talking about it as contract. It recognizes, however, that the covenant is entered into "for the good of the spouses and the procreation and education of offspring" (canon 1055): they are joint ends which should exist in harmony; neither of them should override the other. A fair assessment of the new law may be that it is more adjusted to the mystery than the earlier one was, but it remains in need of reform in order to reflect unfailingly and consistently the spirit of the Council and the simple beauty of our faith.

To this simple beauty of our faith I wish to return in my last remarks.

Conclusion

St. Ignatius of Loyola in his *Spiritual Exercises* proposes a "Contemplation to attain love." He writes: "I will consider how all good things and gifts descend from above; . . . from the supreme and infinite power above; . . . just as the rays come down from the sun, or the rains from their source."

This is exactly what we have done here: we considered Christian marriage, a saving event, as descending from above; a gift to fragile people. But our contemplation cannot end with that, because there is another movement in the opposite direction: all good things and gifts are also ascending to God, as do all human persons. The earthly journey of married persons, God's chosen people, receives its full meaning from its final goal: it is a return to God, Father, Son, and Holy Spirit.

From this perspective, another chapter in the theology of marriage could be written. Or, perhaps, this is the point when all theologians should fall silent and let the mystery speak for itself.

Carlo Rocchetta

5 MARRIAGE AS A SACRAMENT TOWARDS A NEW THEOLOGICAL CONCEPTUALIZATION

*A*t the present time, the debate on the theology of the sacrament of marriage is focused on a variety of issues. Some questions are typically dogmatic in nature: what do we mean to say, as theologians, when we refer to marriage as a "sacrament"? Others reflect the urgent need for new answers from the point of view of pastoral theology, in view of the proliferation of "irregular situations." Other issues, finally, arise in relation to the need to develop a pastoral of marriage that can lead prospective and actual marriage partners toward a fresh realization of the particular identity of their vocation. The complexity of the debate becomes more evident when one considers the difficult situation that the theology of marriage has inherited from the past. Manuals of theology, while appearing to offer a complete doctrinal synthesis, were, in fact, rather poor in substance. The argumentation was almost entirely controversialist in nature, concerned with defending Catholic belief on marriage rather than with deepening its positive understanding.

To this general consideration must be added the almost exclusively juridical and moralistic thrust of theological thinking on marriage, in particular from the end of the Council of Trent until a few decades ago. In works of theology, the study of marriage was often included in the juridical section[1] and, in any event, limited to the consideration of the institution of the sacrament by Christ, and of points of matter and form, of the minister and the subject, following an approach that bore the imprint of canon law rather than that of the sources of revelation. This being the case, it is not surprising that a true and proper spirituality of conjugal life was almost entirely missing. The conception of Christian perfection, modeled on the monastic ideal, was applied *tout court* to marriage between baptized persons, so that the spirituality of the couple came ultimately to be presented as an ascetic upward effort, away from the blandishments of the world, rather than sacrament as a full realization of the sacramental nature of the marriage. Research on the theology of marriage as a sacrament is still today a sort of "fragmented theology," carried on by isolated authors individually, rather than within a common framework making for a unified, global synthesis.

The present paper, of course, does not pretend to solve a situation of this kind. Its purpose is merely to provide an overall picture of the problems involved, and to trace the *main guidelines* for a new theological conceptualization of marriage as a sacrament. For joint consideration at this symposium, I shall identify three main areas for reflection: 1) the sacrament of marriage as *vocation,* 2) the sacrament of marriage as *consecration,* 3) the sacrament of marriage as *communion.*

---

1. See, for instance, G. van Noort, *De Sacramentis*, 2 vols. (Hilversum, Neth.: n.p., 1930). After dealing at length with first six sacraments, all he has to say about marriage is, "Marriage is not dealt with in this treatise because amongst us, as in many other centres of learning, the whole study of marriage takes place in the courses on Canon Law" (Vol. 2,127).

The Sacrament of Marriage as Vocation

The first point to be considered is the vocational identity of the sacrament of marriage; an identity that is rooted in the anthropological structure of the Christian matrimonial event. The sacrament is not something that takes place *beyond* or *above* the polarity of male and female gender, of the man-woman relationship, their love and their mutual choice, but *within,* inside that situation, as a covenant that takes place "in the Lord," and transforms the earthly reality of marriage into a mystery of salvation. It is the very community of love between man and woman that, in the grace of the Holy Spirit, becomes a "sacrament" in Christ and in the Church. The importance of this fact becomes particularly clear if one looks, for a moment, at the approach inherited from the past.

The weight of the past

As is well-known, traditional reflection on marriage, as gradually developed in the Middle Ages and, in particular, in the post-Tridentine period, is characterized by an essentially contractual conception of the institution. The identity of the sacrament of marriage is defined in terms of a "contract." A contract, in turn, involves three fundamental elements: its object, its ends, and its intent. The object of the marriage contract is the mutual *ius in corpus,* understood as the possession, in a physical sense, of sexual rights on the body of the spouse ("conjugal debts").[2] The ends are those already taught by St. Augustine: *bonum prolis, bonum fidei,* and *bonum sacramenti,* even though the relative order of importance of these is not made

---

2. The idea of "conjugal debt" was so prevalent in traditional canonistic thinking as to be considered more binding than any property right so that it was even considered unnecessary to go to court in order to obtain execution (cf., for instance, Thomas Sanchez (+1610), *De Matrimonio,* lib. 2, disp. 22, no. 13).

immediately clear. The intentional nature is the same as requested in the stipulation of any other contract. Less clear is the question of the *contract-sacrament* relationship. Up until the Council of Trent, positions remained unclear. After the Council, and the position adopted by R. Bellarmine, the thesis that became prevalent was that there was perfect identity between contract and sacrament.[3]

The whole development of post-Tridentine thinking on the subject bears the imprint of this approach; an approach that, in fact, involves the implicit dissociation of the human love of the spouses from the sacrament of marriage, as if they were two almost parallel realities, existing in juxtaposition. If indeed the essence of marriage is that of a contract, then it is inevitable that the sacrament of marriage should end up by being understood as a reality which is juxtaposed from outside onto the dynamics of the spouses' commitment in mutual love, without regard to the deep, inseparable reciprocity and interdependence of marriage and sacrament. Moreover, since the Council of Trent had directed its attention primarily to marriage *in fieri,* and had identified the essence of marriage in the element of mutual consent, theology tended to consider the sacramental nature of marriage as a transient act that is exhausted in the celebration of the marriage contract itself. The *traditio-acceptatio iuris in corpus* thus became not only the object of the marriage contract, but *the structural form of the sacrament itself* with a consequent impoverishment of the theology of marriage as a sacrament which has had a considerable impact on all subsequent thinking. At this point, it is inevitable that the theology of marriage should transfer its attention from the analysis of marriage as a contract to the consideration of its *functions.* Although in principle it is still held that *bonum fidei* represents the main end of marriage, *bonum prolis* becomes, in fact, the primary, if not the only, end or purpose of marriage.

3. See Robert Bellarmine, *Disputationes de controversiis christianae fidei,* especially 3:727.7, 743.6, 743.9, 777.17.

The sacrament of marriage, rather than having the justification for its existence in itself, finds *its meaning outside itself,* in the generation of offspring. The main *bonum* to which marriage tends is thus distinct from the persons of the spouses. The idea that the mutual love of the spouses, the being two-in-one, represents the primary purpose and the specific essence of the institution of marriage is relegated to a secondary place. Little value is attached to the *bonum sacramenti.* The ecclesial nature of marriage is, in the final analysis, circumscribed to the *bonum prolis:* marriage is a *bonum* for the Church because it provides her with further children. The fact that marriage is in itself, and prior to any activity of procreation, an event in which the spouses realize themselves, and a sign of manifestation and actuation of the Church, *Sponsa Verbi,* is almost entirely ignored.

Vatican Council II: a turning point

In this context, it will be easily appreciated that Vatican Council II represented a turning point. Even though it did not concern itself expressly with the theological conception of marriage as a sacrament, the Council propounded a basic approach distinguished by at least two fundamental novelties: the *personal nature* of the conjugal event and its *ecclesial nature* in the full meaning of the term. Marriage is a vocation rooted in the anthropological structure of the existence of man and woman, in the mutual giving and receiving of one to the other. The pastoral constitution *Gaudium et Spes* explains that the intimate conjugal partnership, established by the Creator and endowed by Him with its own proper laws, implies that the partnership of life and love of the spouses becomes a partnership of grace in Christ and in the Church. This partnership is rooted in the mutual consent of the spouses, described with the biblical term of "marriage covenant," which comprehends the juridical meaning of "contract" but includes far richer connotations. *Gaudium et Spes* goes on to say that the content of this

"covenant" lies in the mutual surrender, in the giving and receiving of the partners ("the mutual giving of two persons,"
and therefore not merely "a right on the body") with a view to
their mutual good and the good of their offspring. The content of the married partnership is love, which—in the new
covenant—participates in the love of God for His people, the
Church (*GS* 48,1). "Authentic married love is *caught up* into divine love and is directed and enriched by the redemptive
power of Christ and the salvific action of the Church" (*GS*
48,2).

The formulation of ends still bears, in part, the marks of the
traditional approach, but at the same time it introduces new elements, insofar as it describes the dignity and the value of marriage as a sacrament in terms of a covenant that integrates *from
within* the love relationship of man towards woman and of
woman towards man and, by virtue of baptism, bonds it with
the love relationship that indissolubly links Christ with the
Church. It is on this basis that *Lumen Gentium* places Christian
marriage within the structural dynamism of the Church, the
priestly people (*LG* 10), and of the sacraments and virtues
through which "the sacred nature and organic structure of the
priestly community" is brought into operation (*LG* 11,1). The
celebration of the sacrament of marriage is thus understood as
a manifestation of the common priesthood of the Church and
of the bride and bridegroom. By virtue of this act, the spouses
"signify and share the mystery of the unity and faithful love between Christ and the Church," "help one another to attain ho-
liness in their married life," and "have their own gifts in the
people of God" (*LG* 11,2; *GS* 48, 2–3; *Apostolicam Actuositatem*
11).

Theological inquiry

What are the theological implications of the sacrament of marriage as a vocation that emerge from the Council's position
and from subsequent theological reflection? I shall briefly
enunciate four of them, formulated as theses.

1. The sacrament of marriage as the bringing of the man-woman relationship into the compass of the relationship between Christ and the Church

The sacramentality of marriage takes up and fulfills the love of the two spouses and is not simply superimposed upon it. It is, in fact, from within that love and its dynamism that God brings about a greater love, similar to that which He has for His Church. It is therefore the actual love relationship between the two spouses in the fullness of their persons, of their gender-identified physical nature, and of their giving themselves in a mutual pledge that the "marriage covenant" becomes a sacramental mystery of grace.

This divine love not only respects the otherness of "man" and "woman" but gathers it into itself and leads it to its fullness. The reality of the sacrament of marriage, in fact, receives the person that is man and the person that is woman in their mutual relationship, male and female, one facing the other, and acts thus in one way in the woman and in another way in the man, the woman in her womanliness towards the man, the man in his manliness towards the woman. It is the encounter of love of two human beings, man and woman, that becomes a sacrament; it is the relationship of these two persons which becomes a "sacrament" in the strict sense of the word.[4]

The reason why a sacrament is "needed" for this man-woman encounter to be fully realized lies in the fact that, since the Christian is radically consecrated to Christ in the Holy Spirit through baptism, only Christ may give him or her to another person, and it is only in Him and His Church that the supernatural bond and the condition of grace can come into operation, so that the two spouses may truly and entirely belong one to the other. This is why the original and fundamental minister of the sacrament of marriage is the glorious *Kyrios* and, in Him,

---

4. Among contemporary theologians, Edward Schillebeeckx has drawn particular attention to this aspect of marriage. See especially *Le mariage est un sacrement* (Bruxelles-Paris: n.p., 1961) and *Het Huwelijk: Aardse werkelijkheid en heilsmysterie* (Bilthoven, Neth.: H. Nelissen, 1963).

His ecclesial body. The conjugal event, as a sacrament, is a manifest realization of the love of the Redeemer who, by an act of the Church, gives a man to a woman and a woman to a man, in the full reality of their love and life, so as to unfold in them the mystery of His new and eternal covenant and, through them, proclaim it to the world.

2. *The sacrament of marriage as a fundamental actualization of the Church,* "Sponsa Verbi"

In consequence, the sacrament of marriage is not to be understood as something that the Church performs from the outside on two individuals but as an event in which the Church manifests her specific nature as a fundamental, indestructible, and eschatologically victorious sacrament of the grace of God brought to humankind in Jesus Christ. In every marriage celebration—as in every sacrament—the Church realizes herself in relation to the vital situations of human existence.[5] The spouses are made capable of ontological participation in this ecclesial self-realization by virtue of their baptism. As baptized persons they are in a position to carry out an act that, in its specific ecclesial form, is an act proper to Christ. And it is precisely as an act of Christ that marriage as a sacrament is a manifestation of the ministerial function of the Church, and the ministerial nature of the spouses falls within that broader ministerial compass. Each one of the two spouses gives him or herself to the other one, so that they may be, to each other, the sign of Christ's love for the Church, and of the Church's love for Christ.

The love relationship between man and woman thus finds its origin and its exemplary nature in the mystery of the covenant of Christ with the Church and is perennially nour-

---

5. Karl Rahner has, to his credit, highlighted this aspect. See especially *Kirche und Sakramente* (Freiburg: Herder, 1961); and "Die Ehe als Sakrament," in *Geist und Leben* 40(1967): 177–95, reprinted in *Schriften zur Theologie,* vol. 8 (Einsiedeln, Switz.: Benziger, 1967), 510–40.

ished therefrom (Eph. 5:21–33). As baptized persons, the spouses perform and relive in themselves what is proper to the Church, namely that she is the sign of the irrevocable covenant that Christ offered to the world. At the ontological level, this capacity flows from the nature of baptism and at the personal level, from the free consent of the spouses.

3. The sacrament of marriage as baptismal con-vocation which finds its meaning and fulfillment in the Eucharist

The baptismal consecration, understood as a "being in Christ" is in fact the necessary and sufficient condition for the love between a man and a woman to be taken up by Christ within His marital bond with the Church, participating therein and becoming its efficient sign. The "being in Christ" conferred by baptism is not an "as if" but a real and objective "being in." The sacrament of marriage represents, thus, for the spouses, the putting into practice of one and the same baptismal identity: the sacrament of marriage is *a baptismal convocation.* Through their marriage, the spouses participate no longer as individuals, but as a couple, in the paschal event that realizes the covenant of Christ with the Church; and they accept—in consequence—to be placed, vocationally speaking, in the same dimension of *mutual oblation.* Marriage as a sacrament is offered as an act that calls upon the spouses to relive in themselves the mystery of Christ's paschal oblation and gives them the capacity to do so. This is the theological significance of the freely given, bilateral, and ecclesial consent required by the rite. It is not just a matter of a juridical fact but the commitment to a mutual "yes" that is bonded to the paschal covenant of Christ with the Church and calls for openness to its forming power. The "yes" of the spouses becomes part of the "yes" of Christ to the Church; it establishes them within it and involves them, as spouses, in an essentially paschal spirituality.

To celebrate the Christian rite of marriage is, in fact, for the spouses, a form of surrender of themselves as a couple, to the dynamism of the paschal process, so that the whole of their conjugal existence becomes a paschal event. This makes clear the theological significance of the fact that the celebration of a marriage usually takes place within the context of eucharistic celebration: the meaning of the matrimonial event is revealed and accomplished, in a perennial manner, by the mystery of the Eucharist. Indeed, if the Eucharist consists in the offering of Jesus Christ, Who gives Himself to the Church, Christian marriage is a mode of implementation of this offering and its projection in history. In the mutual gift of one to the other, the spouses agree to put into practice a reciprocal donation modeled exactly after that of Christ in the Eucharist, and thus they manifest and realize, for their own part, the mystery of the Church as the bride of Christ. The communion with the *Kyrios* of the Eucharist is the constant actualization of what marriage signifies and produces in the spouses. There is therefore a twofold relationship: the Eucharist is a sacramental manifestation of the essence of Christian marriage, while Christian marriage represents a form of "realized Eucharist."[6]

4. The sacrament of marriage as the epiphany and historical realization of the love of God for humankind

As a "real symbol" of an ecclesial gesture that causes the spouses to participate in the love of Christ for His Church, the sacrament of marriage constitutes a sign in history of the irrevocable love of God for humankind. The paschal event represents, in fact, the culmination of a divine love that wants to manifest itself and to unfold in the hearts of all human beings. The two spouses are the concrete, historical sign of divine love revealed in Jesus dead and resurrected. The sacrament of marriage thus expresses in its full depth the structural unity that exists between the order of creation and the order of salvation.

Christian marriage realizes in itself this unity which corresponds to the unity of the *mysterion* (in the Pauline sense), pro-

6. See among many studies, the article by A. Ambrosiano, "Matrimonio ed eucaristia," *Asprenas* (Naples) 2–3 (1975): 203–19.

claims it in action, and unfolds it in the world. Just as there are not two kinds of history but only one single history of salvation, starting with the Creation and aiming at a new heaven and a new earth, just so there are not two kinds of marriage: there is only one marriage which is gathered into the reality of Christ's marriage with the Church. The *novitas* of marriage as a sacrament lies in the inclusion of the spouses in the covenant of the Lord in His glory with His bride. This inclusion brings about the transcendental opening up of man and woman as a couple and raises the two spouses beyond their natural possibilities toward the infinite love of God for them and for humankind. The spirituality of Christian marriage has a fundamental connotation: it is not an abstract spirituality, floating halfway between heaven and earth, but rather a deeply human spirituality, rooted in history, that can integrate the living experience of man and woman and turn it into a sign of God's design of love for humankind and a privileged instance of its coming to be. The vocational nature of marriage as a sacrament must be seen within this context of totality: a vocation that is, for this very reason, a *mission*.

The Sacrament of Marriage as Consecration

By placing marriage within this context, contemporary theology makes the point that Christian marriage is, at one and the same time, *memory, presence, and prophecy* of the *mysterion* in the world. The spouses *recall* God's marital love for humankind, they *relive,* "here and now," what this love has given to the world, and they *await and anticipate* the definitive manifestation of God's love in the Heavenly Jerusalem. This means that it is necessary to move on from consideration of marriage as vocation to the deeper level of marriage as consecration, thus developing a new, richer understanding of the sacramental sign, so as to progress from the sacramentality of consensus to the sacramentality of the entire conjugal existence.

The sacramental sign: the traditional view

The scholastic conception of the sacramental sign of marriage is characterized, as is well known, by the hylomorphic structure of matter and form (of Aristotelian origin). This conception has caused considerable difficulties whenever attempts have been made to explain what was the "matter" and the "form" of the sacrament of marriage. According to some authors, matter would be represented by the bodies of the two partners, and form by the words they exchange in making the mutual pledge. Others believed that the matter of the sacrament was to be found in the inward mutual consent, and the form in the words used to formulate it. The problem of the sacramental sign—never clearly solved—involves the issue of the identity of the minister of marriage in relation to the spouses themselves, and this led eventually to the formulation of a solution which became ultimately prevalent throughout the West. In fact, if matter and form are identified with the marriage contract, it inevitably follows that the spouses are to be considered as the only ministers of marriage. It is in them that the sacramental sign (matter and form, however understood) is to be found, and they are therefore the ones who mutually "receive" and "administer" the sacrament to each other. The priest is only a qualified witness (*testis spectabilis*). Toward the middle of the sixteenth century, however, Melchior Cano abandoned this view and maintained that the sacrament of marriage is not to be entirely identified with the marriage contract. Taking up again the thesis of some early Italian scholastics, Cano states that the mutual consent of the spouses constitutes the matter, and the priestly blessing the form of the sacrament and that, consequently, the priest is the minister of the sacrament.[7]

Cano's work was published in 1563, during the Council of Trent and some years after his death. His thesis was favorably

---

7. Melchior Cano, *De locis theologicis libri duodecim*, 8.5.

received by a number of theologians, both during and after the Council.[8] It did not, however, prevail. The introduction, by the Council of Trent, of a canonical form of celebration that provided for the marriage to take place in the presence of the parish priest and of at least two witnesses, tended rather to strengthen the conviction that the spouses were to be considered as the only ministers of the sacrament of marriage. According to the teachings handed down in manuals of theology, this is what was in the minds of the Council fathers when they affirmed the sacramental nature of Christian marriage. It is true that Benedict XIV, in the first half of the eighteenth century, was still willing to permit free discussion of the issue, allowing the plausibility of Cano's view.[9]

After the contrary position adopted by the Congregation of the Council, however, and the condemnation of Nuytz by Pius IX, as well as repeated statements by subsequent pontiffs up to Pius XII,[10] the thesis of the ministeriality of the spouses became a doctrine which was generally accepted,[11] except by most German theologians of the early nineteenth century.[12]

8. See, for instance, W. Estius (+1613), in *IV Sent.* d. 26; F. Sylvius (+1649), in *Suppl.*, q. 42, a. 1, q. 1; F. Toletus (+1596), *Instructio sacerdotum*, lib. 7, c. 2; and H. Tournely (+1729), *De matrimonio*, q. 5, a. 2, t. 2, 63.

9. *De Synodo diocesana*, lib. 8, c. 13, no. 4.

10. Pius XII, in *Mystici corporis*, speaks of "coniuges sibi invicem sunt ministri gratiae," *Acta Apostolicae Sedis* 35 (1943): 202.

11. Just by way of example, I would recall A. Verhamme, "De materia et forma sacramenti matrimonii," *Collationes Brugenses* 48 (1952): 12–16, and "De ministro sacramenti matrimonii," *Collationes Brugenses* 48 (1952): 82–89. According to Verhamme, "the matter and the form of the sacrament of marriage, whatever they may be, must be sought in the contract itself" and, since the sacrament is identified with the contract, "the priest's blessing is in no way an essential part, neither as matter nor as form" ("De materia," 12–13). "Marriage, on account of its special nature, has as its ministers the marriage partners themselves. The spouses mutually receive and administer the sacrament; the priest, on the other hand, is not a minister, but only a qualified witness" ("De ministro," 83).

12. In the 1960s, Pierre Adnes adopts a more flexible position. In *Le mariage*, (Tournai, Belg.: Desclée, 1963), after pointing out that the only text of the magisterium in which the spouses are referred to as ministers is *Mystici*

The need to rethink

The need to rethink this view has been highlighted in recent decades in various theological quarters. The hylomorphic schema of matter and form is ill-suited to the structure of marriage as a sacrament, since it does not make clear how the mutual *traditio-acceptatio* of the spouses can, in itself, be a sacramental event.[13] Taking his inspiration from a text of St. Thomas Aquinas, J. M. Aubert states that for this schema to be acceptable "it would be necessary to place the equivalent of form in the baptismal character, which transform the conjugal situation according to nature (matter) into a sacrament."[14] But even with this kind of explanation, it is clear that there are difficulties involved in applying philosophical categories such as those of matter and form to an act such as marriage as a sacrament. At the most, this can be done only by way of analogy.[15] It is therefore necessary to adopt a broader conception.

---

corporis, he agrees that the priest may be described as the minister of the marriage celebration in the view of the Church. (Italian translation under the title of *Il Matrimonio* (Rome: Desclée, Ed. Pontifici, 1966), 147–53.)

13. Already in the fifties, Michael Schmaus admitted that it was difficult to apply the concepts of matter and form to the sacramental sign of marriage: "It will therefore be better, in the sacrament of marriage, to refrain from applying the concepts of 'matter' and 'form'." *Katholische Dogmatik: Die Lehre von den Sakramenten,* 6th ed., Vol. 4/1. (Munich: n.p., 1964), 80.

14. J. M. Aubert, "Foi et sacrement dans le mariage: A propos du mariage de baptisés incroyants," *La Maison-Dieu* 104 (1970): 123. A similar position can be found in Klaus Reinhardt, *Ehe-Sakrament in der Kirche des Herrn* (Berlin: Morus Verlag, 1971), with further stress on the role of baptism: "The baptism of the spouses has, for the sacramentality of their marriage, a function similar to that of the word as expression of faith in the case of other sacraments" (32).

15. This seems to be the case with S. Teichtweier, "Die Ehe als Sakrament in der Sicht des Zweiten Vatikanischen Konzils," in *Funktion und Struktur christlicher Gemeinde,* ed. H. Pompey and H. Hepp-Mielenbrink (Würzburg: Echter, 1971), 207–17. Teichtweier takes conjugal love with all its component elements as the sacramental sign: the form would be found in the marriage consent, which includes the consent to sacramentality; the matter would be the *una caro* as close communion of life (211).

*1. Ministeriality of the spouses as ministeriality in Christ and
in the Church*

At the moment when a man and a woman engage in a mutual "marriage covenant," they represent symbolically—in their full personal "male" and "female" realities—the mystery of Christ and of the Church. As baptized believers, they perform an act that is, properly speaking, an act of Christ and of the Church and that, as such, signifies and operates an effective introduction of the two spouses, man and woman, into the mystery of the Christ Church covenant. This means that the sacramental sign is provided by the *conjugal community* itself, that is to say by the community of a man and a woman who proclaim their intention to be mutually bound as husband and wife with specific reference to their being "in the Lord," that is to say, being two baptized persons. Their act (since they exist in Christ through the operation of baptism) is the efficacious sign of the paschal *eschaton* of the *Kyrios,* celebrated by the Church in the power of the Holy Spirit. The description of the spouses as "ministers" is therefore to be understood in a broad sense, and not in the sense—as is often claimed—that "the spouses administer the sacraments to each other," as if the sacrament were something that is mutually exchanged, or as if the action of the Church were of a secondary or merely supplementary nature.[16]

The sacraments are acts of Christ and of the Church. If marriage is a sacrament, it is first and foremost an act of Christ and of the Church. The ministeriality of the spouses consists in their participation (by virtue of baptism) in the act of Christ and of the Church, which is symbolically operative with the gifts it signifies. The spouses do not "administer to each other," nor do they merely "receive" the sacrament of marriage as if it

16. It is regrettable that the new *Catechism of the Catholic Church,* published in 1992, should continue to state that "it is the spouses, as ministers of the grace of Christ, who mutually confer on each other the sacrament of marriage. . . ." (no. 1623). A very unfortunate formulation.

were a "thing," but they celebrate an act that—by virtue of their baptism—makes them participants in the mystery of the covenant which takes place for them and in them. From this point of view, to reduce the role of the ordained minister to that of a mere "qualified witness" does not seem to be enough. The nuptial blessing pronounced by the ordained minister was the original form of marriage celebration among Christians. Perhaps it would not be a bad idea to restore the fullness of its meaning as well, instead of reducing it to a sort of appendage of the marriage rite proper, as is the case at present. This kind of rethinking, of course, means that it is necessary to overcome the reductionist conception, which identifies the contract entirely with the sacrament, and to move toward a view that is truly appreciative of the "mystery" of marriage, which would also be closer to that of Oriental theology.[17] "In the West, the stress is placed on the baptismal character of the spouses and on their royal priesthood," notes Cardinal Godfried Danneels. "The priest, as representative of Christ and of the community, publicly confirms the act of the spouses. . . . In the East, the stress is placed rather on the priestly ministry of the priest. . . . Through the person of the celebrant, the Church enters 'visibly' into the constitution of the sacramental sign."[18]

The importance of rediscovering marriage as a *mysterion* is to be seen within the global context of the encounter between the Western and the Eastern traditions. In our language, Christian marriage is customarily referred to as a "sacrament." A term that, according to its etymology, denotes a hidden, divine reality, operating in and through a visible sign. Contemporary theology believes that this term can only be fully understood in relation to its Greek equivalent of *mysterion*. As is well known, a *mysterion* is not simply a hidden or incomprehensible truth but

17. See Godfried Danneels, "Les ministres du sacrement du mariage," in *Mariage et sacrement du mariage,* ed. Pierre de Locht, (Paris: Le Centurion, 1970), 199–207.

18. Ibid., 206ff.

rather the event of God's communication of Himself, which becomes the history of salvation and gift of grace to humankind. The sacraments belong to this category of *mysterion*, and they are salvific acts of the Lord in His glory, which render actual, in the time of the Church, the *ephapax* of the paschal event. It is in this sense that they are described as *mysteria*, "salvific mysteries."[19] Marriage as a sacrament has to be seen in the same light. The supernatural element cannot be conceived as something that is simply superimposed upon the natural order, but rather as something that, while transcending that natural order, takes it up *ad intra*, raises it up, and leads it to its fullness.

2. *The sacrament of marriage as a "consecrating sacrament"*

Reasoning along these lines, it becomes clear that one of the main challenges to theological thinking in our time is the need for a deeper understanding of marriage as a "permanent sacrament." The Council of Trent did not go further than to recall that the grace of the sacrament of marriage "perfects conjugal love, confirms the indissolubility of this love and sanctifies the spouses."[20]

It was Robert Bellarmine who, in relation to the scholastic distinction between *matrimonium in esse* and *matrimonium in fieri*, introduced the idea of the *permanent sacrament* by analogy with the sacrament of the Eucharist: "The sacrament of marriage may be considered in two ways: firstly, while it is being celebrated; secondly, as long as it lasts after it has been celebrated. And this because it is a sacrament similar to that of the Eu-

---

19. Regarding the importance of this understanding, I should like to refer, among many other relevant studies, to Raphael Schulte, "Die Einzelsakramente als Ausgliederung des Wurzelsakramentes," in *Mysterium Salutis*, vol. 4/2, (Einsiedeln, Switz.: Benziger, 1973), 46–155. For a more detailed analysis, see Carlo Rocchetta, *Sacramentaria fondamentale: Dal "mysterion" al "sacramentum,"* 2d ed. (Bologna: Edizioni Dehoniani, 1990).

20. "Amorem perficere, indissolubilem unitatem confirmare, coniugesque sanctificare" (*DS* 1799).

charist, which is a sacrament not only while it is being performed, but as long as it endures. In consequence, as long as the spouses live, their union is always a sacrament of Christ and of the Church."[21] This splendid intuition, however, remained an isolated insight and was not incorporated into the mainstream of official theology. What continued to prevail there was the view of marriage as a contract which we have already discussed.

The matter was only taken up again three centuries later by Matthias Joseph Scheeben.[22] He believed that the sacrament of marriage could be described, just like baptism, confirmation, and holy orders, as a "consecrating sacrament." According to Scheeben, consecrating sacraments are those through which "we are consecrated to a supernatural task and come to occupy a special and permanent position in the mystical body of Christ."[23] The consecration is operative in the supernatural bond between the two spouses, within the supernatural bond that exists between Christ and the Church—a bond that is an irradiation of, and a participation in, the permanent bond that unites human nature with the divine nature of the Word.[24] The prevalence of neo-Scholasticism in theology prevented Scheeben's views from exerting much influence until after the publication, in 1930, of Pius XI's *Casti Connubii*. That encyclical, quoting the above-mentioned text of Bellarmine, stressed how the spouses, by virtue of the sacrament of marriage, are "sanctified and strengthened in the duties of their estate by means of a special sacrament, the efficacious virtue of which, although it

21. Robert Bellarmine, *Disputationes de controversiis, III; De Matrimonio, controversia II,* c. 6.

22. Matthias Joseph Scheeben, *Die Mysterien des Christentums,* 2d ed. (Freiburg: Herder, 1865). Reprinted in *Gesammelte Schriften,* 2d ed., vol. 2, ed. Josef Höfer, (Freiburg: Herder, 1951).

23. *Die Mysterien des Christentums,* 471.

24. "Thus, Christian marriage, by its very nature, amounts to a supernatural consecration, and the spouses themselves are consecrated to God in a particular manner and enter thus into a special union with Christ and with His life of grace" (Ibid., 472).

does not impart character, is nevertheless permanent."[25] The Pope speaks there of "quasi consecration," comparing the sacrament of marriage to that of baptism and of holy orders.[26] Later manuals of sacramental theology have succeeded only in part in making clear the richness of this statement.[27]

Vatican Council II, on the other hand, made explicit reference to the permanence of Christ with the spouses, and to their "quasi consecration" (*GS* 48,3). The Council did not state in so many words that marriage is a "permanent sacrament" but implied as much when it made clear that the foundation of Christ's permanence with the spouses is to be understood in the sense of a spousal covenant in line with God's covenant with the chosen people and with the definitive covenant established by Christ with the Church (*GS* 48,3). *Familiaris Consortio*, in no. 13, seems to refer to a similar conception when it explains that, regarding salvation, "the spouses participate both together, as a couple, to such an extent that the first, immediate effect of marriage (*res et sacramentum*) is not supernatural grace itself, but the Christian conjugal bond, a twosome communion which is typically Christian because it represents the mystery of the incarnation of Christ, and of His mystery of covenant."[28] This supernatural bond, by analogy with the char-

---

25. *Acta Apostolicae Sedis* 22 (1930): 553.

26. Ibid., 555.

27. F. Sola, for instance, deals with the problem of the permanent sacrament on the basis of its nature as a contract. A contract is a transient, not a permanent, reality: "What endures in the marriage is a bond, but this is not the contract itself, but its effect or consequence," "De matrimonio," in *Sacra Theologia Summa*, vol. 4, (Madrid: BAC, 1954), 746–8. (This is a new edition, revised and amended, of the original text of 1943.) The text of Pius XI is commented upon as follows: "The Pope propounds these things as *piam considerationem* and not as *doctrinam*, and for this reason they do not need to be given preference over the opposite view" (Ibid., 746). A similar attitude, albeit expressed in a more differentiated and cautious manner, is found in most authors, at least up to the sixties and seventies.

28. This explanation in *Familiaris Consortio* is based on the classic tripartite analysis of the sacrament: marriage, in its sign (*signum tantum*), has as its first and immediate effect the conjugal bond (*res et signum*), and to this is added as

acter of the three sacraments that confer it, may be qualified as a *quasi character*. "Quasi," not in the sense that it is something inferior to "character" proper but in the sense that it is an actual manifestation of God's irrevocable covenant in relation *to the two spouses* who are thus raised to a new sacramental union in Christ and in the Church. It is *the consecration of the union of two persons* and not of one single individual. The spirituality of marriage is thus the actual expression of a sacramentality that not only involves the whole of the conjugal community but calls the spouses to communion and to sanctity in the totality of their existence (*sacramentum permanens*). It is not only just the consent that is a sacrament but the whole existence of the spouses united "in the Lord."

3. The fertility of marriage as a sacrament: beyond simple biology

It is in this context that the full meaning of the fertility of a couple's life, beyond the purely biological level, must be seen. Conjugal life is the image of God the Creator, not primarily through the activity of procreation, but because it is a *union* that constitutes the living form of self-giving in love, disinterestedness, communion, and service. It is because of this that conjugal life is an image of God the Creator. It is not primarily, or exclusively, a matter of physical fertility. Otherwise animals, with their fertility, would also be an image of the divine activity of creation, while infertile spouses would not!

Conjugal fertility lies, above all, in the unitive and total love which makes it possible for the spouses to develop in mutual growth, following the model of the Creator and of the love of Christ for the Church, in a reciprocal flow of exchange, of giving and receiving, which leads the spouses to serve, with the whole of their existence, God's design of love for the world. Procreation itself finds its full significance only within the framework of a love which the spouses develop and which has the capacity of signifying the creative action of God as an ex-

---

a second effect the supernatural grace (*res tantum*), as a consequent gift and its requirement.

pression of love in the mutual readiness of the spouses to serve each other and to serve life.[29] The concept of matrimonial fertility, within the context of marriage as a sacrament, is to be understood in this richer meaning as "obedience to the deep inner dynamism of love" and as "the gift of oneself to others," to use the language of *Familiaris Consortio* (no. 41).

The Sacrament of Marriage as Communion

This brings us to the third aspect: *The sacrament of marriage as communion*—a communion that has its source in the ineffable communion of the Trinity, unfolds it and makes it manifest in the process of history. This aspect has not often been given much attention in theological discourse. Only in recent decades have a few attempts been made to pursue this line of thought, and even these start off from widely different assumptions.

Recent attempts

Karl Barth, for instance, sees in Genesis 1:27 the statement that the human couple was created "in the image of God" not simply as a reference to their ability to procreate but as meaning that the couple reflect and reproduce in themselves that relationship between "I" and "You" that constitutes the Divine Being itself. "The characteristic feature," he writes, "of the essence of God, which consists in being an 'I' and a 'You', and the characteristic feature of the human person, which consists in being 'man' and being 'woman', correspond exactly to one another."[30] As a matter of fact, Scheeben had already attempted to develop a Trinitarian understanding of the concept of

29. A beautiful description of this kind of fertility is found in *Apostolicam Actuositatem* 11, where, by way of example, reference is made to the adoption of children, the harboring of foreigners, contributions to the education of the young, catechetical service and financial aid furnished to engaged or married couples who find themselves in material or moral difficulties, assistance to the elderly, etc.

30. Karl Barth, *Die Kirchliche Dogmatik*, vol. 3/1 (Zürich: EVZ, 1945), 41, 2.

the human couple, created in the image of, and similarity to, God,[31] and had gone so far as to suggest that the creation of Adam symbolized the eternal generation of the Word and the creation of woman symbolized the procession of the Holy Spirit, thereby communicating, according to Greek theology, from the Father through the Word, as an exemplary manifestation, beyond the fact of creation, of permanent relationship between man and woman: man representing the Word, God's creative strength and power, and woman the Holy Spirit, God's love and tenderness.[32]

Scheeben's and Barth's approaches are suggestive enough, but they have been criticized for lacking adequate exegetical foundations. For this reason, some authors today tend to seek the basis for the duality of gender and for the conjugal communion not so much in a human analogy with the mystery of the Trinity but rather in the nuptial relationship existing between Christ and the Church.

This is, for instance, the position of the "later" Herbert Doms,[33] who maintains that the *why* of the creation of the human couple can only be understood in the light of redemption. The human couple, according to him, has been created by God in the image of Christ and of the Church, as seems to be suggested in Ephesians 5.[34]

Need for a new approach

These attempts are certainly not without merit. The problem, however, at least as far as we are concerned, is to avoid ab-

---

31. Matthias Joseph Scheeben, *Handbuch der Katholischen Dogmatik*, vol. 3 (Freiburg: Herder, 1972) 148, nos. 368–74.

32. Ibid., no. 375. Cf. also M. Valkovic, *L'uomo, la donna e il matrimonio nella teologia de M. J. Scheeben* (Rome: Pontificia Universitas Gregoriana, 1965).

33. The "earlier" Herbert Doms adopted the same position as Scheeben; cf. *Vom Sinn und Zweck der Ehe* (Breslau: Ostdeutsche Verlagsanstalt, 1935). See French translation: *Du sens et de la fin du mariage* (Paris: Desclée, 1937), 30.

34. Herbert Doms, "Zweigeschlechtlichkeit und Ehe," in *Mysterium Salutis*, vol. 2 (Einsiedeln, Switz.: Benziger, 1967). See Italian translation: "Sessualita e matrimonio," in *Mysterium Salutis*, vol. 4 (Brescia: Queriniana, 1970), 419–24 and 447.

stract speculation and to proceed on the basis of the specific fact of marriage as a sacrament as a result of the operation of the Holy Spirit, Who makes the couple who marry in the Lord into a living "shrine" of the Trinity.

The Holy Spirit and marriage

The first point to be recalled in this connection is the pneumatological dimension of marriage as a sacrament.[35] The Holy Spirit is the invisible protagonist of the marriage between two baptized persons in its entire vocational reality, as "consecrating sacrament" and as communion. It is in the Holy Spirit that man and woman meet and build one another in love. It is in the Holy Spirit that they present themselves to the Church and celebrate their marriage. It is in the Holy Spirit that their mutual consent is made actual in the "yes" of Christ and the Church and makes them partners in the new covenant. It is in the Holy Spirit that the spouses exercise their baptismal priesthood and realize their conjugal community of love and of grace. There is no step on the conjugal path that is not under the sign of the Holy Spirit.

It is not by accident that rituals both before and after the Council of Trent provided for the celebration of a "Mass of the Holy Spirit" as an act of preparation for the marriage rite proper. This was intended to recall that the sacramental event of marriage flourishes in the Church as a gift of the Holy Spirit. Even today, in the Oriental churches, the climax of the marriage ceremony consists in the placing of crowns on the heads of the bride and bridegroom as a symbol of the invocation of the Holy Spirit and of His descent onto the spouses.[36] Not only

35. *Familiaris Consortio* says: "The Spirit that the Lord pours forth renews the heart and makes it possible for man and woman to love each other as Christ has loved us" (no. 13). A good contribution to the study of this subject has recently been made by Moises Martinez Peque in his *El Espíritu Santo y el Matrimonio a partir del Vaticano II* (Rome: Antonianum, 1991).

36. The present Catholic rite, unfortunately, is not as rich. In the *editio tipica* of 1969, the Holy Spirit was present in only one of the forms of words proposed for the blessing at the conclusion of the Mass. In the revision of the rite

the rite but the ultimate *res* of the sacramental act is the *donum Sancti Spiritus* as the source and synthesis of all gifts that flow from Christ's work of redemption. The Holy Spirit poured forth on the spouses is the source and principle of the bond that unites them indissolubly and makes them into participants in the "marriage" of Christ with the Church (*Familiaris Consortio*, no. 21) This gift is the basis and foundation of the twofold effect of the sacramental event of marriage: *the permanent bond and the operation of grace.*

The presence and the action of the Holy Spirit represent the root and indestructible nourishment of the life of the spouses and of their mutual giving and receiving. As Paul Evdokimov puts it, in a rather poetic but expressive kind of language: "It is the Spirit that calls forth the priestly charity of the husbands and awakens the motherly tenderness of the wives."[37]

Conjugal life as an event of Trinitarian communion

By virtue of the gift of the Holy Spirit, the existence of Christian spouses reaches out to the depths of Trinitarian communion, thus becoming a "sacrament" and an actual manifestation of the eternal suffusion of the Trinity in history. The Holy Spirit, as the spirit of the love of the Father and of the Son, brings about the supernatural transformation of the love of man and woman, making it part of the Trinitarian Love that constitutes the very being of God. It is not just a matter of an image of the Trinity in the order of creation, as is the case with every human marriage. In the Christian marriage, the Trinity

---

carried out in 1990—in addition to some changes in the prayers of the faithful and in the choice of Biblical readings—an epicletic formula has been introduced, accompanied by the imposition of hands, into the prayer for the blessing of the spouses. This is certainly an important change, but it is still entirely insufficient and inadequate to express the pneumatological dimension of the rite of marriage in relation to its origin, its accomplishment, and its global significance.

37. Paul Evdokimov, *Sacrement de l'amour: le mystère conjugal à la lumière de la tradition orthodoxe* (Paris: Descleé, 1977). See Italian translation: *Sacramento dell'amore: il mistero coniugale secondo la teologia ortodossa* (Brescia: Cens, 1969), 226.

is present, and lives in the "I-you" of the spouses as a manifestation of grace, in a manner that is certainly mysterious, but real,
and that can only be apprehended by faith. The grace be-
stowed at baptism on the individual already effects the presence of the Holy Trinity. In the couple, this presence is effect-
ed in a new manner, as a joint communion of both partners
and their participation in the dynamism of Trinitarian Love.

The Trinity represents the formative source of marriage as a
sacrament of communion. Since the Holy Spirit is the *nexus
amoris* of the Father and the Son, the action of the Spirit in
marriage is expressed as a bond and a reciprocity of love and,
hence, as the foundation for the love of the couple and its development. Thanks to the gift of the Holy Spirit, the whole existence of the spouses is placed under the sign of the mystery
of the Trinity, following a circular movement *(from the Father
through the Son in the Holy Spirit / in the Holy Spirit through the
Son to the Father)* which makes of conjugal existence a living
Trinitarian doxology, within the Trinitarian dynamism of the
Church and the liturgy. The communion of the spouses will
undoubtedly be subjected to trials, difficulties, and tempta-
tions, but the presence of the Spirit will ensure that they enjoy
the assistance of the necessary grace to be able to renew themselves every day in their dedication and love each other as
Christ loved the Church and gave Himself for her sake, forever,
in mutual dedication (*GS* 48). This communion will have to be
nourished day by day, in a dynamic process of reconciliation
and of joy.

Conclusion

Christian marriage can aptly be described in the concluding
words of St. John in the Book of Revelation: "The Spirit and
the bride say: 'Come'. And let him who hears say: 'Come'.
Whoever is thirsty, let him come; and whoever wishes, let him
take the free gift of the water of life" (Rev. 22:1). The presence

of the Holy Spirit is invisible; it operates in silence, but it is a silence overflowing with intensity and vibrations. The *epiclesis* that distinguishes the existence of the conjugal community from its inception will then be characterized by the keeping of that "sacred silence" which alone makes it possible to receive the "inexpressible" language of the Holy Spirit (Rom. 3:29) in listening to the word of God and in prayer. The gift of the sacrament becomes life, and life becomes a sacrament. Truly, as St. John Chrysostom says: "Marriage according to Christ is marriage according to the Spirit: a true spiritual generation."[38]

38. *Homily on the Epistle to the Ephesians,* 20, 5 (*PG* 62, 141).

CONTRIBUTORS

Klaus Demmer, born in 1931 in Münster, Germany, was professor of moral theology from 1961–1965 in Oeventrop/ Sauerland, and from 1966–1970 he was on the Faculty of Theology in Paderborn. Since 1970 he has taught at the Pontifical Gregorian University in Rome. Publications: *Moraltheologische Methodenlehre, Zumutung aus dem Ewigen, Die Wahrheit leben: Theorie des Handeln, Introduzione alla teologia morale.*

Ladislas Örsy S.J., born in 1921 in Hungary, has taught canon law at the Pontifical Gregorian University, Rome, Fordham University, New York, and The Catholic University of America, Washington, D.C. Presently he is visiting professor of Jurisprudence at Georgetown University Law Center, Washington, D.C. Publications: *Marriage in Canon Law: Texts and Comments, Reflections and Questions, The Church: Learning and Teaching. Magisterium, Assent, Dissent, Academic Freedom, Theology and Canon Law: New Horizons for Legislation and Interpretation.*

Carlo Rocchetta, born in 1943 in Prato, Italy and ordained in 1968, holds a licentiate in biblical theology and a doctoral degree in dogmatic theology from the Gregorian University of Rome (1976). He has taught sacramental theology at the *Ateneo Sant'Anselmo* of Rome and at the Gregorian University. He is presently professor in sacramentology at the *Studio Teologico*

Fiorentino in Florence and offers a course in Fundamental Theology at the *Università Cattolica del S. Cuore* of Rome. He has been president of the *Società Italiana per la Ricerca Teologica* (SIRT). Publications: *Storia della salvezza e sacramenti, I sacramenti della fede, Sacramentaria fondamentale: Dal "mysterion" al "sacramentum," Per una teologica della corporeità, "Universa nostra caritas est eucharistia," Il sacramento della coppia.*

Michel Rouche, born in 1934 in Paris, holds his degree in historical studies from the Sorbonne. He has been professor in medieval history at the Charles de Gaulle University (1969–1989), the Sorbonne (1989), and the Catholic University of Paris (1985). Presently he is director of the *Institut de la Famille* of the Diocese of Paris (1986) and president of the journal for marital spirituality, *Alliance* (1979). Publications: *L'Aquitaine des Wisigoths aux Arabes, Histoire de l'enseignement et de l'education, Des barbares à la Renaissance, Alto Medioevo, Clovis.*

Jörg Splett, born in 1936 in Magdeburg, Germany, has been since 1971 a professor in philosophical anthropology and religious philosophy at the *Philosophisch-Theologische Hochschule Sankt Georgen*, Frankfurt, and visiting professor at the *Hochschule für Philosophie* in München. Publications: *Meditation der Gemeinsamkeit* (with Ingrid Splett), *Gotteserfahrung im Denken, Freiheits-Erfahrung: Vergegenwärtigungen christlicher Anthropo-theologie, Leben als Mit-Sein: Vom trinitarisch Menschlichen, Spiel-Ernst: Anstösse christlicher Philosophie.*

BIBLIOGRAPHY

Adnes, Pierre. *Le mariage*. Tournai, Belg.: Desclée, 1963.

Ambrosiano, A. "Matrimonio ed eucaristia." *Asprenas* (Naples) 2–3 (1975): 203–19.

Angelus Silesius. *Sämtliche Poetische Werke*. 2d ed. Munich: Allgemeine Verlagsanstalt, 1924.

Aubert, J. M. "Foi et sacrement dans le mariage: A propos du mariage de baptisés incroyants." *La Maison-Dieu* 104 (1970).

Balthasar, Hans Urs von. *Das Weizenkorn*. 8th ed. Einsiedeln, Switz.: Johannes Verlag, 1958. Translated by Erasmo Leiva-Merikakis under the title *The Grain of Wheat* (San Francisco: Ignatius Press, 1995).

Barley, Delbert. *Hannah Arendt: Einführung in ihr Werk*. Freiburg: K. Alber, 1990.

Barth, Karl. *Die Kirchliche Dogmatik*. Vol. 3/1. Zürich: EVZ, 1945. Translated by G. W. Bromiley under the title *Church Dogmatics* (Edinburgh: T. & T. Clark, 1975).

Bellarmine, Robert. *Disputationes de controvesiis christianae fidei*. Prague: n.p., 1711.

Bours, Johannes, and Franz Kamphaus. *Leidenschaft für Gott: Ehelosigkeit, Armut, Keuschheit*. Freiburg: Herder, 1981.

Cano, Melchior. *De locis theologicis libri duodecim*. Salamanca: n.p., 1563.

Casel, Odo. *The Mystery of Christian Worship*. London: DLT, 1962.

Corbett, Percy Ellwood. *The Roman Law of Marriage*. Aalen, Ger.: Scientia, 1979.

Danneels, Godfried. "Les ministres du sacrement du mariage." In *Mariage et sacrement du mariage*, edited by Pierre de Locht, 199–207. Paris: Le Centurion, 1970.

Doms, Herbert. *Vom Sinn und Zweck der Ehe*. Breslau: Ostdeutsche Verlagsanstalt, 1935.

———. "Zweigeschlechtlichkeit und Ehe." In *Mysterium Salutis*. Vol. 2. Einsiedeln, Switz.: Benziger, 1967.

Evdokimov, Paul. *Sacrement de l'amour: le mystère conjugal à la lumière de la tradition orthodoxe*. Paris: Descleé, 1977.

Faivre, Alexandre. *Les laïcs aux origines de l'Eglise*. Paris: Le Centurion, 1984.

Frisch, Max. *Gesammelte Werke in zeitlicher Folge*. Vol. 2. Frankfurt am Main: Suhrkamp, 1976.

Girard, René. *La violence et le sacré*. Paris: B. Grasset, 1972. Translated by Patrick Gregory under the title of *Violence and the Sacred* (Baltimore: Johns Hopkins University Press, 1977).

Grootaers, Jan. *Le chantier reste ouvert: Les laïcs dans l'Eglise et dans le monde*. Paris: Le Centurion, 1988.

Guardini, Romano. *Welt und Person: Versuche zur christlichen Lehre vom Menschen*. 2d ed. Würzburg, Ger.: Werkbund-Verlag, 1940. Translated under the title of *The World and the Person* (Chicago: H. Regnery Co., 1965).

Hildebrand, Dietrich von. "Die Bedeutung von Mann und Frau füreinander außerhalb der Ehe." In *Die Menschheit am Scheideweg*, 127–45. Regensburg, Ger.: Habbel, 1954.

Léon-Dufour, Xavier. "A Cana, les noces de Dieu avec Israel." In *Lecture de l'évangile selon Jean*. Vol. 1, 203–45. Paris: Seuil, 1988.

Lies, Lothar. *Sakramententheologie: eine personale Sicht*. Graz, Aust.: Styria, 1990.

Martinez Peque, Moises. *El Espíritu Santo y el Matrimonio a partir del Vaticano II*. Rome: Antonianum, 1991.

Mazza, Enrico. *Mystagogy: A Theology of Liturgy in the Patristic Age*. Translated by Matthew J. O'Connell. New York: Pueblo Pub. Co., 1989.

Örsy, Ladislas M. *Marriage in Canon Law: Texts and Comments, Reflections and Questions*. Wilmington, Del.: M. Glazier, 1986.

———. *Theology and Canon Law: New Horizons for Legislation and Interpretation*. Collegeville, Minn: Liturgical Press, 1992.

Rahner, Karl. "Die Ehe als Sakrament." In *Geist und Leben* 40(1967): 177–95. Reprinted in *Schriften zur Theologie*. Vol. 8, 510–40. Einsiedeln, Switz.: Benziger, 1967.

———. *Kirche und Sakramente*. Freiburg: Herder, 1961.

Reinhardt, Klaus. *Ehe-Sakrament in der Kirche des Herrn*. Berlin: Morus Verlag, 1971.

Rocchetta, Carlo. *Sacramentaria fondamentale: Dal "mysterion" al "sacramentum."* 2d ed. Bologna: Edizioni Dehoniani, 1990.

Saint-Exupéry, Antoine de. *Gesammelte Schriften*. Vol. 3. Munich: dtv, 1978.

Sanchez, T. *De Matrimonio*. Antwerp: n.p., 1642.

Scheeben, Matthias Joseph. "Die Mysterien des Christentums." In *Gesammelte Schriften*. 2d ed. Vol. 2. Edited by Jösef Höfer. Freiburg: Herder, 1951.

————. *Handbuch der Katholischen Dogmatik*. Vol. 3. Freiburg: Herder, 1972.

Schillebeeckx, Edward. *Het Huwelijk: Aardse werkelijkheid en heilsmysterie*. Bilthoven, Neth.: H. Nelissen, 1963.

————. *Le mariage est un sacrement*. Bruxelles-Paris: n.p., 1961.

Schmaus, Michael. *Katholische Dogmatik: Die Lehre von den Sakramenten*. 6th ed. Vol. 4/1. Munich: n.p., 1964.

Schulte, Raphael. "Die Einzelsakramente als Ausgliederung des Wurzelsakramentes." In *Mysterium Salutis*. Vol. 4/2, 46–155. Einsiedeln, Switz.: Benziger, 1973.

Sola, F. "De matrimonio." In *Sacra Theologia Summa*. Vol. 4, 746–8. Madrid: BAC, 1954.

Splett, Jörg. *Freiheits-Erfahrung: Vergegenwärtigungen christlicher Anthropo-theologie*. Frankfurt am Main: Verlag J. Knecht, 1986.

————. *Leben als Mit-Sein: Vom trinitarisch Menschlichen*. Frankfurt am Main: Verlag J. Knecht, 1990.

————. *Lernziel Menschlichkeit: Philosophische Grundperspektive*. 2d ed. Frankfurt am Main: Verlag J. Knecht, 1981.

————. *Spiel-Ernst: Anstösse christlicher Philosophie*. Frankfurt am Main: Verlag J. Knecht, 1993.

Teichtweier, S. "Die Ehe als Sakrament in der Sicht des Zweiten Vatikanischen Konzils." In *Funktion und Struktur christlicher Gemeinde*. Edited by H. Pompey and H. Hepp-Mielenbrink, 207–17. Würzburg: Echter, 1971.

Valkovic, M. *L'uomo, la donna e il matrimonio nella teologia de M. J. Scheeben*. Rome: Pontificia Universitas Gregoriana, 1965.

van Noort, G. *De Sacramentis*. 2 vols. Hilversum, Neth.: n.p., 1930.

Verhamme, A. "De ministro sacramenti matrimonii." *Collationes Brugenses* 48 (1952): 82–89.

————. "De materia et forma sacramenti matrimonii." *Collationes Brugenses* 48 (1952): 12–16.

Wickler, Wolfgang, and Uta Seibt. *Männlich Weiblich: Der grosse Unterschied und seine Folgen*. Munich: R. Piper, 1983.

INDEX

adultery, 28, 34, 35
affection, 13, 34, 36
Agoult, Marie, 35
androgyneity, 20
Aristophanes, 17
Aubert, Jean-Marie, 67
Augustine, 27, 29, 57

Balzac, Honoré de, 34
Barth, Karl, 75, 76
Beauvoir, Simone de, 36
Bellarmine, Robert, 58, 71
Benedict XIV, 66
Bernard of Clairvaux, 30
body, 14, 57, 60, 66
bonum fidei, prolis, sacramenti, 57–59
Bossuet, Jacques Bénigne, 32
bride, bridegroom, 22, 28, 35, 42,
    43–44, 45–46, 47, 51, 60, 64,
    75, 77
Buber, Martin, 22

Cano, Melchior, 66
Casti Connubii, 72
Cathars, 30
celibacy, 30, 31
Charlemagne, 29
Chatelet (Marchioness du), 33
children, 15, 20, 25–32, 40, 41, 42,
    46, 50, 59

Christ-Church relationship, 42,
    59–62, 63, 70–71, 73, 74
Chrysostom, John, 76
Churchill, Winston, 35
coitus interruptus, 32
Colette, Gabrielle, 36
communion, 51, 56, 64, 71, 73–77
concubinage, 26, 27, 28
condilectio, 22
consecration, 8, 59, 63, 65–74
consent, 26, 27, 31, 32, 34, 36, 58,
    59, 63, 66, 74
contract, 49, 57–58, 59–60, 66, 69,
    71
Council of Trent, 9, 31–32, 56, 57,
    58, 66–67, 71, 77
covenant, 8, 42, 45, 53, 59–65, 69,
    73
creation, 13–14, 39–43, 49, 64–65,
    74–76

Danneels, Godfried (Cardinal),
    70
Delille, Jacques, 34
Denis (Madame), 33
divorce, 26, 34–36
Doms, Herbert, 76
Douai, Merlin de, 34
dowry, 26, 28, 35
Durkheim, Emile, 13

ecclesia domestica, 6, 47, 50
Evdokimov, Paul, 78

Familiaris Consortio, 6, 73, 75, 78
family, 2, 5, 13, 25, 26, 28, 32, 34,
    36, 44, 47, 48
father, 15, 25, 37
Feydeau, Ernest, 35
fidelity, 7, 8, 33, 35, 36, 40, 44
Francis de Sales, 31
freedom, 14, 18–19, 27, 34–37
Friedelehe, 28
friendship, 15, 26, 27
fulfillment, 17–18, 21, 24

Gaudium et Spes, 8, 53, 59–60
gender, 14–15, 20, 57, 61, 74
gift of oneself, 18–19, 64, 74
grace, 40, 44, 49, 57, 59, 61, 71,
    73, 78, 79

happiness, 21, 27
homosexuality, 30
Hugh of St. Victor, 29
humanity, 15, 45
husband, 13, 25, 26, 27, 28, 32, 33,
    35, 69, 78

Ignatius of Loyola, 53
image of God, 39, 74–75, 78
infidelity, 8, 36
Innocent I, 29
Isidore of Seville, 29
I-Thou relationship, 16–19, 75–76
Jansenism, 32
Jean de Meung, 30
Jesus, 42, 47, 62, 64, 65
Jonas of Orleans, 29
justice, 20–21, 49
Juvenal, 26

Laclos, Pierre Choderlos de, 34
law: canon, 9, 47–49, 56; civil, 9,

29, 35, 36, 47–48; Roman,
    25–26, 27, 30, 48
Liszt, Franz, 35
liturgy, 8, 50–51, 79
Lothair II, 29
Louis the Pious, 29
love, 8, 9, 10, 12, 16–20, 21, 27,
    28, 29, 33, 35, 53, 74; conjugal,
    9, 16–20, 21, 29, 33, 43, 46,
    57, 58, 59, 60, 61–62, 74, 75,
    77, 78; courtly, 30; divine, 8,
    30, 31, 46, 59, 60, 61, 62, 64–
    65, 78; free, 33–34, 35, 36
Lumen Gentium, 60
Luther, Martin, 30–31

Marcus Aurelius and Faustina,
    27
Marivaux, Pierre Carlet de
    Chamblain de, 33
Maupassant, Guy de, 35
ministeriality, 67–71
misogyny, 30
missio canonica, 11
modesty, 18
monogamy, 26, 28–29
Morgengabe, 28
mother, 15, 25, 26, 27, 30, 34
Mund, 28
Musonius, 26
mystery, 3, 9, 17–18, 24, 52, 63,
    70, 76; of marriage, 38, 52, 63,
    63–64, 70–71

Newman, John Henry (Cardinal),
    48
Nicolas of Cusa, 20

offspring, 15, 26, 41, 52, 59, 60
oneness, 17, 19–21
Other, the, 16–20
Ovid, 26

Paetus and Caecina, 27
partnership, 2, 14, 39, 52, 59
passion, 26, 31, 32, 33, 35
Peter Lombard, 30
Philemon and Baucis, 27
Pius IX, 67
Pius XI, 5, 72
Pius XII, 67
Plato, 17
pledge, 19, 21, 61, 66
Plutarch, 26
polygamy, 25, 29
prayer, 4, 31, 51, 80
priest, 12, 29, 32, 34, 44, 45, 51,
    66, 70
procreation, 15, 19, 31, 49, 59,
    74–75
promise 12, 19, 42, 45, 50
puritanism, 26, 31, 34

Racine, Jean Baptiste, 32
redemption, 45, 46, 51, 76, 78
remarriage, 29, 32, 35
Richard of St. Victor, 22
Roland (Madame), 33
Rousseau, Jean-Jacques, 33
Rufus, 26

sacrament, 8, 10, 11–12, 39, 42, 44,
    47, 60, 61, 68, 69; of baptism, 3,
    12, 42, 44, 47, 60, 61, 68, 69; of
    marriage, 2, 3, 9, 11–12, 31, 32,
    39, 42–43, 47, 55–80; of the
    Eucharist, 12, 47, 63, 69; per-
    manant sacrament, 69–71
Sade (Marquis de), 34
Saint-Exupéry, Antoine de, 16
Saint-Lambert, Jean François de,
    33
salvation, 12, 51, 57, 64, 71

Sartre, Jean-Paul, 36
Scheeben, Matthias Joseph, 72,
    76
Schopenhauer, Arthur, 17
self, the, 16, 16–19
self-realization, 3, 18, 62
self-revelation of God, 8, 24
Seneca, 26, 33
sexuality, 5, 9, 20–21, 26, 27, 30,
    31, 34, 57
shame, 18, 27
Song of Songs, 16, 30
spirituality, 4, 30, 48–49, 64; of
    marriage, 3, 6, 36, 48–50, 56,
    64, 73–74
Stoicism, 26–27
symbol, 30, 43, 44, 49–50, 64, 75,
    76

Teutberge, 29
togetherness, 13, 17, 19, 21
Trinity, 9, 12, 47, 72, 73, 74,
    75
Tristan and Isolde, 28
trust, 19, 53
truth, 21, 22, 23, 48, 49, 71

Vatican Council II, 8, 9, 50, 53,
    59–60, 73
Vincent of Beauvais, 29
vocation, 2, 3, 6–7, 9, 11, 12, 49–50,
    55, 57–65
Voltaire, 33
vows, 34, 44, 45

Wagner, Richard, 17
wedding feast of Cana, 42, 51
wife, 13, 26, 28, 35, 69, 78–79

xeirothesia, 45, 50

Christian Marriage Today was designed and composed in Baskerville with Alcuin display type by Kachergis Book Design, Pittsboro, North Carolina; printed on 55-pound Natural Hi-Bulk and bound by Braun-Brumfield, Inc., Ann Arbor, Michigan.